I JUST CAN'T STOP IT

Roger Charlery
1963–2019.

I JUST CAN'T STOP IT

MY LIFE IN

RANKING ROGER
WITH DANIEL RACHEL

OMNIBUS PRESS

London / New York / Paris / Sydney / Copenhagen / Berlin / Madrid / Tokyo

I had a connection to The Beat – I cut two records with them in the Eighties and had the best time: their lyricism, charm and energy were part of my growing up. Watching them smash the audience to bits during the David Bowie *Glass Spider* tour was one of the highlights of my life – and always – Ranking Roger and Dave Wakeling up front: one toasting, one singing... and getting it just right. Saxa blowing like a hurricane...

Roger's story is one of struggle, fame and survival. Enjoy...

Sir Lenny Henry

The mid Seventies was one of the most influential periods in the history of British pop music. The merging of Caribbean rhythms and the tropes of the immigrant West Indian experience alongside young white bands struggling to find an identity in Thatcher's disunited kingdom produced what would become the second wave of British dominance in popular music across the world.

My friend Roger, as a founding member of The Beat, was at the centre of this febrile and explosive clash of cultures, uniquely placed to document the excitement of those times, the heady joy of success, the political turmoil, the inherent racism at all levels of our society as well as the brotherly bond of musicians struggling to make themselves heard within it.

It's a great read. We need more skanking from Ranking.

Sting

I first met Ranking Roger on the doorstep of Jerry Dammers' house, a short while before I saw him perform with The Beat at an early Selecter show in Birmingham. He was very young, sweet sixteen, but his gangly, youthful frame and mischievous grin, coupled with a joyous light that seemed to shine from his every pore, made such an impression on me that I have never forgotten that moment. As we both simultaneously reached for the doorbell, little did we know that both of our lives would become irrevocably changed by 2 Tone.

Forty years have passed since that moment, but one thing has remained constant, Roger's light has never dimmed. When he steps on stage it's as though he is lit from within. I have seen this light dazzle audiences who've come to see his many high energy, rhythm driven performances with The Beat; music that embodies love, joy and unity.

It has been a total honour to have shared so many worldwide stages with this talented and profoundly spiritual man in recent years. May his light forever shine.

Pauline Black, lead singer of The Selecter

CONTENTS

AUTHOR PLAYLISTS

Playlists available on Spotify.

Punk and new wave playlist compiled by Ranking Roger of The Beat
1. Sex Pistols – 'Anarchy In The UK'
2. The Clash – '(White Man) In Hammersmith Palais'
3. Buzzcocks – 'What Do I Get'
4. X-Ray Spex – 'Identity'
5. Devo – 'Jocko Homo'
6. Iggy Pop – 'The Passenger'
7. Kraftwerk – 'The Model'
8. The Fall – 'It's The New Thing'
9. Adam & The Ants – 'Zerox'
10. Bow Wow Wow – 'C·30, C·60, C·90 GO'
11. Generation X – 'Ready Steady Go'
12. Sham 69 – 'Borstal Breakout'
13. The Damned – 'New Rose'
14. The Police – 'Roxanne'

15. Siouxsie & The Banshees – 'Hong Kong Garden'
16. Dead Kennedys – 'Holiday In Cambodia'
17. Au Pairs – 'Come Again'
18. The Cure – 'Killing An Arab'
19. Joy Division – 'Love Will Tear Us Apart'
20. Ruts – 'Staring At The Rude Boys'

Reggae playlist compiled by Ranking Roger of The Beat
1. Dave & Ansel Collins – 'Double Barrel'
2. Eric Donaldson – 'Cherry Oh Baby'
3. Black Uhuru – 'Guess Who's Coming To Dinner'
4. Tapper Zukie – 'MPLA'
5. Big Youth – 'Screaming Target'
6. Misty In Roots – 'Mankind'
7. Steel Pulse – 'Handsworth Revolution'
8. Burning Spear – 'Marcus Garvey'
9. Dennis Alcapone – 'Spanish Amigo'
10. General Saint & Clint Eastwood – 'Another One Bites The Dust'
11. Dillinger – 'Marijuana In My Brain'
12. Lee Perry & Prince Jammy – 'Rude Boy'
13. Rupie Edwards – 'Ire Feelings (Skanga)'
14. Sheila Hylton with Sly & Robbie – 'The Bed's Too Big Without Me'
15. UB40 – 'The Earth Dies Screaming'
16. Justin Hind & The Dominoes – 'Carry Go Bring Come'
17. Lloydie & The Lowbites – 'Birth Control'
18. Laurel Aitkin – 'Pussy Price Gone Up'

19. Cedric Myton & The Congos – 'Can't Take It Away'
20. Linton Kwesi Johnson – 'Sonny's Lettah (Anti–sus Poem)'

The best of The Beat playlist compiled by Daniel Rachel

1. 'Mirror In The Bathroom'
2. 'Tears Of A Clown'
3. 'Ranking Full Stop'
4. 'Twist And Crawl'
5. 'Whine And Grine / Stand Down Margaret'
6. 'Save It For Later'
7. 'Hands Off… She's Mine'
8. 'Best Friend'
9. 'Jeanette'
10. 'I Confess'
11. 'Drowning'
12. 'Doors Of Your Heart'
13. 'Too Nice Too Talk To'
14. 'Spa Wid Me'
15. 'Two Swords'
16. 'Get-A-Job'
17. 'Big Shot'
18. 'Ackee 1-2-3'
19. 'Can't Get Used To Losing You'
20. 'Who Dat Lookin''

Bonus tracks

1. Beat Man [previously unreleased Beat demo]
2. Inna England [previously unreleased Beat demo]

INTRODUCTION:

Noise in This World

'Stop your fuckin' fighting,' I screamed. 'Have you come here to fight or dance? Look. I'm a black man.'

I ripped off my hat and jacket.

'See, I'm black! So what you here for?'

There were a half dozen or so skinheads in the audience shouting 'Sieg Heil' and National Front slogans. We'd only played three songs. My blood was boiling and I was about to jump into the audience when Dave Wakeling grabbed me.

'Don't let them get to you, Roger.'

Suddenly, from nowhere, the rest of the audience started chanting, 'Black and white unite.' We launched into 'Whine And Grine', an old Jamaican song, written by the founding father of ska, Prince Buster. The infectious rhythm of the music simmered down the fraught atmosphere but an underlying unease hung in the air. There was a racist minority and the majority of the audience didn't know how to react and looked to me on stage with the microphone to do something. Deanne Pearson reviewed the gig in the *New Musical Express*, and said, on this occasion, I was 'almost hysterical with rage and emotion'.

I was becoming familiar with skinheads spitting or throwing coins at me. Beat shows were designed to take an audience to the maximum. But it soon became apparent that the faster tunes likes 'Click Click', 'Two Swords' or 'Noise In This World' could start a riot. The intensity of those songs had a very powerful effect on an audience, whereas slower grooves like 'Rough Rider' and 'Big Shot' would have a calming effect. My usual tactic was either to ignore racist provocations or to try and reason with the antagonists. But a couple of times it got out of hand and I couldn't hold myself back. The fighting and abuse at gigs cemented my mission to promote a message of peace, love and unity. I realised troublemakers would taunt you, but they wouldn't touch you, so I began to toast my response *love and unity the only way*. I brought that into The Beat.

I would ask myself, 'Why are skinheads throwing coins?' I reasoned that it was to do with confusion and the music changing. By 1979 punk had mellowed and merged with pop. And the fashion changed. It felt like, as a rebellion against new wave, punks became skinheads or rude boys. Then you ask yourself, 'What is the difference between a skinhead and a rude boy?' It's about quarter of an inch in your hairstyle. Yet, despite the subtle sartorial differences, both tribes shared the same musical tastes. Certainly, original skinheads from the late Sixties loved reggae music and understood street culture, but the second generation, the late-Seventies incarnation, didn't realise that a lot of the music they danced to was made by black people. As unlikely as it seems, a lot of skinheads didn't make that connection until later in life. I've met former skinheads who used to spit and throw coins at me who have thanked me for The Beat changing their lives and said, 'Your music made me realise it wasn't about colour.'

In the wake of Enoch Powell's inflammatory 'Rivers of Blood' speech in 1968, when he said, 'In this country in fifteen or twenty years' time the black man will have the whip hand over the white man,' I always felt my status in England was under threat. British law could change at any time and deportation became an ever-present fear. My parents had come to England – Dad in 1959, Mum in early 1961 – with the plan to work for five or ten years and save enough money to go back to St Lucia with their children. That was the mindset of the majority of Caribbean people who came to work in post-war England. But the system never paid enough. All the families I knew in our neighbourhood were just hanging on. Mum eventually made it back home, but it took her the best part of forty years.

In 1977, Andrew Brons stood as a National Front candidate in the Stechford by-election, where I grew up, and polled more than 8 per cent of the vote, pushing the Liberal contender into fourth place. I had first become aware of the National Front a few years earlier when their racist pamphlets started appearing through our family letterbox. Stechford, in East Birmingham, was home to the headquarters of the National Front and they would regularly march past our house, shouting their racist slogans. 'Go home, you black bastard.' I would follow them on the roadside, and yell back, 'I was born here, mate.' We were right in the middle of it. The blatantly bigoted chants and prejudiced banners were frightening but in a show of community solidarity neighbours would come out on the street and shout and swear at the marchers. Their outrage, and courage, to stand up to racism, made me feel protected.

There would be larger marches in the city centre every few months, of maybe two or three hundred National Front supporters. Inevitably, a counter demonstration would be organised and the Front would be confronted by three thousand anti-racist campaigners, spearheaded by the Anti-Nazi League and Rock Against Racism. I would say, 'Where are all the black people, man?' I soon realised it was a representation of how the country was on a bigger scale; that the majority of white people were against right-wing extremists.

The National Front march in Digbeth on February 18, 1978 was a big one. The police tried to make the anti-fascist demonstrators go a separate way from the official march but they somehow ended up meeting the Front and all hell broke out. I thought, 'Right, time to go.' If there was ever any trouble at protests I would be out of there. That wasn't what I'd come for. I was there to demonstrate, not fight. And realistically any police officer would look at me as a black guy, first and foremost, and that would mean trouble. The footage from the Digbeth riot was used in the opening sequence of The Clash film *Rude Boy* before their gig at Barbarella's later that night, and gives a good impression of the tensions amongst youth on the streets in late-Seventies Britain. It's funny to think that within two years of that day I would be not only friends but performing on stage with The Clash, who to my mind were the greatest punk band of all time. By then I had become a pop star, toured the world and played a small part in the biggest youth movement since punk rock.

Part One:
The St Lucian Connection

The Rub-Up

Upbringing. St Lucia. School

I was born Roger Charlery on February 22, 1963, at 51 Grantham Road in Sparkbrook, less than two miles from Birmingham city centre. I didn't have a middle name. Mum said I was called 'Roger' after the actor Roger Moore. My dad was a big fan of the television series *The Saint*, which was first broadcast on October 4, 1962, the day before the first Beatles single, 'Love Me Do', was released. We lived in my uncle's house and Mum and Dad rented a room from him when they first came to England a few years earlier. It was a big four-bedroom house and we had one room downstairs; four of us in one room. You may have thought after my sister, Equilar, was born in 1961 that these sleeping arrangements would have acted as a natural form of contraception. They didn't. I came along two years later. The house belongs to my auntie now and I have always felt that there is something important about the property. I was born there and I wouldn't mind dying there. The house number '51' is significant too: 5 + 1 = 6. I've noticed a pattern in my life of '6's, and '7's: flight numbers and hotel rooms I stay in always add up to six or seven; I was born on the 22nd day of the 2nd month: 2 + 2 + 2 = 6. The Beat's first hit single, 'Tears Of A Clown', peaked at number six in the UK charts. I feel comfortable when I see a six or a seven. I see them as good numbers.

My parents, Anne Marie Louison and John Baptist Charlery, met around 1957 in St Lucia, a French-speaking island in the Caribbean, where they had two daughters Sandra (b. 1958) and Annie (b. 1960). Greta, my half-sister, was born to a different father in 1955. St Lucia is a Catholic island. The British and the French ruled there for over four hundred years. Seven times British. Seven times French. It gained independence in 1979. Twenty years earlier, in 1959, when the British government were calling out to the Empire countries for labour to run the National Health Service and British Rail, Dad came to England followed by Mum in early 1961. They travelled alone and Greta, Annie and Sandra were left with my grandparents; I would be almost four before I met them. In St Lucia, family was tight-knit and everybody looked after everybody else's kids. You would never have a problem with babysitting. Many St Lucians came to London when they arrived in England. I don't know why Mum and Dad settled in Birmingham. All they wanted to do was work and make enough money to bring over their children from the Caribbean.

Dad was a musician. My older cousins would say, 'Your father used to play a mean saxophone. He also played the guitar, but as soon as he came to England he gave it all up to work in a factory.' There was a heavy machine factory in Deritend and all I remember is him saying he worked on a capstan lathe. Dad always used to dress smart in a tie and shirt and jacket. He would say, 'I've come here to make money.' He may have put his instruments away but he remained a total music lover. The living room at home was filled with records and he had an eclectic record collection. It was the first time I ever heard the funk of James Brown or the pop of Manfred Mann or Motown. Dad also listened to a lot of country and western. Artists like Charlie Pride, Jim Reeves, Patsy Cline and Tammy Wynette. I used to love Brenda Lee, especially the saxophone parts. He also used to listen to a lot of African music. I'd get into the catchy rhythms but I didn't have a clue what they were singing about. I don't think Dad brought any records with him from St Lucia. Most of his records were collected in England, probably because most calypso records were pressed in London, before being shipped out to the Caribbean. Records were played on the stereogram downstairs. It had valves so you had to wait fifteen seconds for the large dark wood unit to warm up. It had a great bass sound. We weren't allowed to touch it but music was always in the house.

I first heard ska from Mum, and at parties when I would have been about six or seven. All the relatives took it in turns to have everybody round. We would go to Uncle Henry's every other weekend. His real name was Hesbury, but everybody called him Henry. He had a big detached house in Palmerston Road, which he would open up and blast out calypso and reggae records with the odd country and western tune thrown in. The adults would usher us kids out of the living room so they could dance but it was always exciting to watch them through the crack in the door. There was a dance called the 'rub up' where a male and female would dance pretty close to each other, whining and grining in time to the music. It was very sexy. Along with records like '007' by Desmond Dekker and 'Double Barrel' by Dave & Ansell Collins, I must have heard 'Cherry Oh Baby' by Eric Donaldson a billion times. It was a classic tune and it would be played five times straight. It was a perfect tune for the 'rub up'. The parties would go on till two or three in the morning. We would fall asleep in one of the upstairs bedrooms and in the early hours be woken and have to struggle back home, half asleep.

When I was about four years old my parents sent me and Equilar to St Lucia. They wanted to save up enough money to bring all five of us back, 'To live,' as they used to say, 'a better life in England.' I wasn't old enough to appreciate their sacrifice or to even understand why Mum and Dad weren't coming too. We were simply told we were going to live with Grandmother and then we would come back to England with our sisters. That was a shock in itself – 'I've got three more sisters!' How you take that in as a four year old, I don't know.

I don't recall much detail about the voyage to the Caribbean except Equilar and I had a guardian allocated to us and I remember being lifted up onto the boat by a stranger. I was scared because of the water and I was crying. The man said, 'You'll be all right.' On the ship we were handed these strange-tasting eggs. I didn't know what they were but they tasted wonderful. All the kids slept together in a huge room and we were all given a toy and a small bag of sweets. I ate all of mine straightaway and at night I got out of the bunk in the dormitory we all shared and walked around to this other boy's bed. He hadn't touched his sweets so I swapped my empty bag with his full one. It was my first taste of crime, but not my last.

When we docked in St Lucia, where we would spend the next eighteen months, Equilar and I met our sisters, Greta, Annie and Sandra, and grandparents, Laura and Frederick 'Pedro' Augustin, for the first time. There are two big families in my history, the Moneros and the Augustins. Mum and Dad were clearly black but my maternal great grandmother was fair skinned. Grandmother could understand English, but she didn't speak it and she would speak in her broken French. My great grandfather, Pa Deveaux, was a comedian. He played banjo and sang songs that would have people in stitches. Everywhere Pa Deveaux went people knew him. He would write songs about folks he encountered and make them laugh by making things up out of the top of his mind. That was something special. I'm told it's from him I get my cheekiness and perhaps my ability to ad-lib on a microphone.

Ma and Pa Deveaux lived in a wooden house and although there was electricity and running water it was one of the poorer properties on the island. My biggest memory was the night of the great hurricane. The whole house was shaking and you could hear bashing and see great sheets of lightning illuminating the sky. I really wanted to open the front door and go outside. I distinctly remember an adult saying, 'Don't open the door because there is someone out there and they'll take you away.' In my head the hurricane became a person.

I cried a lot for my parents. I was bought a brown and white puppy who I called Lucky. It made me really happy because I had a friend. Not that I was lonely; there were lots of other kids to play with in the area. I started school and my best friend was a boy called Lodger. Everywhere we went, it was, 'Here's Roger and Lodger.' When I went back to St Lucia when I was about nineteen, they said, 'Do you recognise that man, over there? That's Lodger.' I'm over six foot but this guy was smaller than me and had dreadlocks all the way down to his feet. He was looking at me out of the side of his eye. Then he said, 'Wha'ppen,' and it was big hugs. As kids we used to fight each other all the time but apparently we were inseparable.

I distinctly remember the smell of St Lucia. It was a pungent odour of green and earth. It was unlike anything I'd ever experienced in England. It was most likely a combination of scents from the banana and coconut and palm trees. And the air was really thick and musty. The Windward Islands get a lot of rain but it's really hot as well. The rain would come and then within about ten minutes it would be as dry as a bone and you would have thought it had never rained. On the same trip I reunited with Lodger I had diarrhoea after stupidly drinking unclean water – before I arrived there had been a drought and mosquito eggs and bacteria had collected in the dry water tanks. Once it started raining the fresh water was contaminated. Auntie Ta instructed people to get the plant the goats ate together with a collection of herbs and then she boiled them to make a medicinal tea. I suppose she was what we call an herbalist. Auntie Ta was Mum's eldest sister and my favourite auntie. Despite her age she was still hip and was in with the young ones. All the other aunts and uncles were very heavily against marijuana, but once in a while Auntie Ta would have a smoke. She was on our generation's level. She listened to country and western and merengue. She was one of the personalities in the family. Auntie passed away in 2017.

Dad grew up in Malgretoute by the sea about three miles away from Micoud, where Mum and Dad first met. When I was about nineteen I went to the village to visit Grandmother, Ma Eliwick, and some of my relatives and to learn about my culture and history. Malgretoute was more or less all bush; underdeveloped and full of mosquitoes; a small village of no more than fifty houses made out of either tin or wood or sometimes brick for the larger dwellings. There were a few stores but the nearest church was a good five mile walk along the dirt road. Grandmother lived in a house that had been built for her

by her sons and we sat and she held my hand the whole time.
I looked so much like Dad it would have been very emotional
for her. While I was there I met many cousins. Coming from
England, I was seen as a money magnet. I had to show that I
was still well-balanced and as normal as them. People would
expect me to buy small things, like a round of drinks, which I
happily would. But then I'd say, 'Come on, let's see your money,
then.' Of course, I'd spent a lot of my earnings on the air flight
just to get there. One of my cousins was called Shellos. He took
me to the top of the big hill with a magnificent view of the sea.
During my visit I heard so much musical talent and began to
imagine building a studio and releasing records for the people
of St Lucia. Shellos said, 'All of this land belongs to the family.
You could build wherever you want.' Then I started thinking,
'Yeah... until the hurricane comes!'

I remember very little about leaving St Lucia and returning
to England. It was 1968 – I was five years old – and we flew
back on a BOAC. We were entranced to be on a plane and
as we descended over London I remember looking out of the
window and not knowing what the houses were. Equilar said,
'They look like rows of tin cans.'

All of a sudden there was seven of us all living in England.
We lived on the top floor of a house on Claremont Road in
Sparkbrook with a front room and a narrow corridor which
led to a kitchen and a bedroom. It was crammed. My four
sisters and I shared one room and Mum and Dad used the

front room. From the landing, staircases led downstairs where some African people lived. Mum threw a party to celebrate our return from St Lucia but we weren't allowed to stay up because it was too late. We lived in Claremont Road for about a year but I don't have any memories of adjusting to life back in England. Or even the fact that Equilar and I now had three older sisters living with us. Children are very resilient to change and my life happily trundled on.

When I was about seven or eight we moved to Cattell Road in Small Heath, and a year later Dad left Mum. I was nine years old. I still don't know why to this day. I've never asked him. I saw him leaving, I grabbed on to him and said, 'Don't go. Don't go.' He said, 'I've got to go. Let go of me.' He kept pushing me away, and saying, 'No, I have to.' A friend of his came and put all his belongings in the back of a van. My last memory was seeing Dad sat in the passenger seat as they drove off.

My parents splitting up must have affected me but I still had Mum and I reasoned there was nothing I could do about it. I was used to Mum and Dad arguing but I hadn't thought anything of it. It was normal for parents to bicker. Although they didn't argue in front of us I would hear them in their bedroom having spats and trying to keep their voices lowered. The house was often filled with the silence between them. Divorce was inevitable, but it took them seven years to actually do it. In the meantime, we still had a good time as a family and their love for us never waned. But Mum would continually cuss Dad under her breath, 'You could have done this… you might have cleaned up that…'

In retrospect, I think Dad must have been fed up or one of them must have been having an affair behind the other's back. Dad certainly had one affair, if not a couple. One of them was with a friend of the family, which I unintentionally discovered when I heard them rowing when I was about seven or eight. The woman was a friend of the family and there was a picture of her in the family photo album. Oddly enough Mum never took it out when she learnt about Dad's infidelity. Mum would never talk about their separation and offered no explanation. She would just simply say, 'Your dad left.' Mum continued to cuss him and we would stay with him at weekends. Later, Dad remarried, and in 2015 I met his new family – my half-sister and half-brother, Sarah and Kevin – at their home in Billesley.

Dad had to get away for his own reasons, and as a young adult I reacted to his departure by subconsciously challenging figures of authority. His leaving gave me a sense of freedom to be mischievous knowing that he wasn't there to tell me off any more. I did a lot of naughty things. I once took a piece of wood from the coal fire and used it as a poker to set fire to the back of Sandra's dress because she had wound me up. Fortunately, just as the flames were beginning to take hold, they were extinguished by one of my other sisters and Sandra wasn't hurt. I was given such a beating. It wasn't that I was angry in myself, it was more to do with testing boundaries and learning new barriers. Dad had been very strict and was always on my case. It is possible that had he stayed with Mum I would never have joined The Beat. As it was, I walked out on Mum to get away from her and our deteriorating relationship. I had to become a stereotype before I could shape up and change my ways. I had to go out into the wilderness and find out about life and make my own mistakes.

When I was about fifteen I stole a couple of mod shirts from a shop on Bull Street. I had a coat on – I stuffed the shirts inside it and zipped it up. I even talked to the salesperson before and after, 'Goodbye,' 'Yeah, see you again.' I kept one shirt and gave the other to a kid who dared me. He was few years older than me and I had met him knocking around in town. He said, 'I can't believe you did it!' It was a one-off. I was misguided and soon after I began to get a bad vibe from him and distanced myself. The incident reminds me of a song we'd later write in The Beat called 'The Limits We Set':

shoplifting my little brother
shoplifting my little sister
said all you got to do is
just a forward through the door
but when they come fe check you out
you no come back for more
tell me which one would you prefer
one hundred pound fine
or three months in prison

me old cock sparra?
shoplifting shoplifting

When I became a father in my twenties I had to ask myself, 'Am I going to be the same as my parents and beat my children?' There's a fine line between punishment and learning a lesson. Many is the time I have had to stop myself, and say, 'I don't want to beat my kids.' They've had the odd slap on the back of the legs when they've done something really bad, but I was westernised. I was the next generation. I don't think there's anything wrong with that. It acts as a deterrent so that next time you can use it as a threat, and say, 'Do you want another slap?' I've never used a stick or a belt. Not because of what happened to me but because I see everybody as a human being. One day, when my son, Matthew, was about four or five, I was shouting at him, 'Don't you dare do that!' I felt like beating him. He looked up at me and his eyes welled with tears. I would have looked like a giant to him. I crumbled, 'Oh no. Don't cry.' I grabbed him, pulled him up to head height, and gently said, 'This is why I don't want you to do that. Daddy loves you. I don't want to shout at you. I have to explain it to you.' He took it in and from that day that boy has never been scared of me.

I have five children – Matthew, Leon, Reuben, Lucia and Saffren – and oddly enough, all of them have taken their mother's surname. None of them are Charlerys. Leon, who is now in his thirties, lives in Moseley. He's a hidden gem and very much like me. He writes music in so many different styles: from pop and jazz to old rocker and dub style. Saffren has added vocals to Beat records. And when Matthew – aka Murphy – was fifteen he got involved with the reformed Beat as 'Ranking Junior'. The songs were second nature to him so all he had to learn was the dance moves. At first he thought they were crazy but now he does the same ones as me. His involvement in The Beat also prompted a new role for myself as lead vocalist, while Murphy took over the toasting and the harmonies. I didn't expect him to do it exactly the same as me, and while it's similar he does it in his own way with a different attitude. A lot of people couldn't have the same job as one of their parents but when it comes to music, Murphy and I join together. He's always my son but he's also my best mate. He's part of the team and we respect each other. I've always said family is like a clan. We have to talk and be open with each other. It's the only way it will work. You can't hide things away from each other. Murphy got that from a young age. It is such a pleasure to have my son performing alongside me. I feel it is like handing down the Beat baton to the next generation. It's a blessing that we have an understanding, even though we have totally different personalities and outlooks. Murphy calls me Radical Roger because I'm always buying gadgets. I've always got the latest thing. In my home I have four robot-style hoovers which operate automatically and clean the room. They go everywhere, under the settee, round tables and chairs, and even up and down the stairs. I have a sensor-activated bin that opens and closes when you pass your hand across its lid, and a similar device that feeds paper towels in the bathroom. Back in the Eighties, I had one of the first MP3 players. I bought it in Tokyo when I was in General Public. You could download six songs onto it. I could have spent £1 million in Japan buying gadgets. I remember a dimmer light that lowered down from the ceiling like a UFO and made a noise like something out of *Close Encounters of the Third Kind*. As a kid I loved weird noises and flashing lights, but I've come to realise I'm attracted to technological innovation and being at the forefront of new commodity trends.

I got beatings from both of my parents when they were together. If I was rude, Dad would slap me or beat me with anything he could lay his hands on. Mum would whack me with a strap or a wooden stick or a metal bar; whatever was nearest to her. I would regularly get punished for being naughty. It was the same for all the kids round our way. West Indian parents are very strict. I remember going back to St Lucia when I was about nineteen; I saw a big man in the village being beaten by his mother. He would have been in his twenties but he wouldn't have dared lay a finger on her because she had brought him into this world. As big a man as he was, she was putting him right. It's a different social mentality to the British way.

One day, Mum couldn't beat me any more because by then I had learnt boxing and Aikido. I said, 'All right, you can try and beat me but I'll block you.' I was defending myself and saying, 'Mum you don't have to do this.' She tried to hit me but couldn't make contact. It was frustrating for her. Eventually she got really angry and walked out the room, went downstairs, and said to one of my uncles, 'You see! Roger's trying to do karate on me now.' She stopped beating me after that; but she could still shout. Up until she passed away, she would still say, 'I can still beat you, y'know.' I loved Mum for that. She tried to put me right. I respected her but sometimes I was right too, and that's where we clashed. When The Beat made money I would get a lump sum of £20,000 from the record company and give her £5,000, or say, 'Here's £10,000 for the house in St Lucia for when you retire.' She would take it, and say, 'That's for all the troubles you've given me over the years.'

I had a weird relationship with Mum. I loved her to death but as I grew older I found I couldn't reason with her like other mothers and sons seemed to. She had her way of thinking and I had my own. Maybe it's because she was an Aries and I am a Pisces. Part of the problem, I think, was because I was the youngest, and her only son. She had always wanted a boy. She had all those girls and then finally, with me, she had her wish. The problem was it meant I was spoilt. Everything was done for me. Or I would be bought more new clothes than my sisters. I'd have a pair of trousers and within a few days the knees would be gone or I'd scuff my shoes until holes appeared in the toe. I was expensive to keep. At dinner time, I would be served an extra portion or Mum would purposely leave some on her plate, and being Mr Greedy, I would look up at her with wide eyes. 'Oh, do you want some of mine, Roger?' It was small things. I had to do housework but I got away with doing less. My sisters would get their revenge and bully me. When I say bullying, it wasn't nasty or physical, I didn't go to my bedroom scarred or depressed. I just got my fair share of it. My sisters would wait until Mum left for work and then make me sweep the floors and do their chores for them while they sat and read magazines. Their nickname for me was Dembo.

I would get the blame for everything. If anything was wrong or broken, 'Roger did it.' When I was about fifteen I had a scrap with Annie. We both went for it. I pulled her about and tugged her. It was a real fight and I've still got a mark on my cheek from a nail scratch. I can't even remember what it was over. I'd had enough of being bullied and being told what to do and I saw red. The fight didn't last very long. The next thing I knew the others came in and broke it up. It could have been one of those things where we didn't talk to each other for years, but after a week or so it was forgotten about. And we never fought again. Most of the time we all got on and would play games around the house and have pillow fights. One of the best times was when we would take the single mattress from our bedroom, put it on the top of the stairs, and slide down when Mum was at work.

Living with four girls introduces an insight to the opposite sex many young boys often miss out on. I used to read all my sisters' magazines, like *Jackie* and *Mandy* and the problem pages. And of course, I always fancied my sisters' friends, but Annie would say, 'I don't want you going out with any of my friends.' I would listen to them talking about boys with their friends and would learn so much about how girls think and operate by just listening. As a contrast to male boisterousness and fighting to decide who is the toughest, I learnt a different way of being. There was a balance to be found from understanding the female point of view. By the time I was sixteen I had developed a strong feminine side to my character, something which a lot of men don't find until their thirties or forties. When I was about eight or nine my sisters painted my face with lipstick and mascara and powder. It was funny but I'm glad we didn't have phone cameras then. Another time I went into Mum's room and experimented with all her different colours and blushers. I was scolded when Mum discovered the mess.

Every weekend we would be sent to Sunday school followed by Mass. I didn't ever see Mum go to church but she still sent us. We used to wag it and go down the park instead. My sisters would make me swear not to say anything and I learnt how to keep secrets from my parents. Mum was a hard worker. She had a small licensed business selling small wares with this guy who had a van; Tupperware and clothes and sweets. They would travel round the area selling street by street. After Dad left home, I think Mum discreetly had other partners, but kept it away from us. I respected her privacy. As an adult, if I go out with someone I don't want the whole world knowing my business. That came from Mum. Mum then got a position as a machine-tool setter, in Tyseley, south Birmingham, making spanners. She worked there for nearly thirty-five years. They loved her. Mum always battled with her health. She had a hard time and was in out of hospital. She had high blood pressure, problems with her back... Diabetes in later life. She had her ovaries removed. She had to take a lot of time off work but they would always have her back. They looked after her. When she retired, before she returned to the Caribbean they had a big goodbye party for her.

Mum never believed I would come to anything. She thought I'd be a failure. We loved each other but we always clashed. It was difficult. Although, she approved when I joined The Beat, believing it was a good thing for me. She met management and members of the band and thought they were good guys. Before a gig they would pick me up in the van and she would wave me off goodbye. As we became more successful there would be pictures of us in the paper but she always treated me the same. I'll never forget the moment Mum saw us on *Top of the Pops* for the first time performing 'Tears Of A Clown'. I saw tears coming out of her eyes and I said to myself, 'Gotcha!'

The last time I saw her was when there was a family reunion in St Lucia. Mum died in January 2013 from a heart attack. I was at home and I received a call from the Caribbean. I was really shocked. Wendy, Mum's niece, was with her at home in Micoud when it happened. It was decided that they would drive to hospital because it would be quicker than waiting for an ambulance; Mum died en route. I flew out for the funeral, which was held in a Catholic church. There were a lot of people there; all the family. I had Saffren, my daughter, to grab on to and hold me firm. I had seen Mum's body at the funeral parlour. My sisters were saying things like, 'Why did you have to go and die on us?' I stood a few feet away for about ten minutes. I didn't touch her. It was a really emotional experience. But Mum got a good send off.

When I was nine we moved to 47 Stuarts Road on the corner of the Bordesley Green East. Stechford was predominantly a white area with a strong Irish community and I started at a Roman Catholic comprehensive called Archbishop Williams. A lot of black families wanted to get their children into a Catholic school to get a good education. It was mixed gender and the majority of the 1,100 children were of Irish descent. There were eleven black kids in the whole school; five in my year. If it had been an English school it would have been a problem; with so few black kids we could have felt threatened. That isn't to say there wasn't some racism. The odd kid might call you a 'black bastard' but the fact that we were outnumbered made us get on with everybody, which we wanted to do anyway.

I got to understand the plight and history of the Irish. As a people, they are more likely to be racist towards the English than towards black people. Both the Irish and black people have been oppressed by the British for hundreds of years. We had a lot in common. A lot of punks were Irish. I think that's why I found my way mixing with them in later years. When the Mulberry Bush and the Tavern in the Town were bombed in 1974 every Irishman in Birmingham was suspected of being in the IRA. I can recall distinctly the sound of the explosions followed by the sirens of ambulances and fire engines. It was chaos. From where we lived we could see the smoke rising up from the city centre and, initially, thought one of the gas mains in Saltley had blown. Then we saw on television that twenty-one people had died and there were 182 casualties. Despite six suspects being arrested within hours, the Irish community came under an enormous amount of pressure. For once, I wasn't the one being pointed at. Typically black people got the blame for everything. We were the nation's scapegoat. It was dangerous walking round town but you still did so with pride. In the wake of the pub bombings, for the first time, my Irish friends understood how I felt. All our parents were working in the same factories, white and black, and they were learning to work out their differences. For us, we shared the same education and went to the same schools. I was born into the system and educated by the system. It was easier for my generation.

Growing up, it was always a big deal to see somebody black on television, especially if they were one of the good guys, like Sidney Poitier. All the family came round to watch him in *Guess Who's Coming to Dinner*. The film was the inspiration for Black Uhuru's song 'Guess Who's Coming To Dinner, Natty Dreadlock', which I have always liked. In the

Seventies there were only three terrestrial television channels and you always had the sense of a nation watching the same programmes. Up to seventeen million people a week would watch *Love Thy Neighbour* and we were amongst the viewers. There was outrage when it was first shown on ITV. The story was based around a black family moving into a suburban house in the Home Counties next door to a working-class white family, with a bigoted husband, Eddie Booth, played by Jack Smethurst. As a family we were used to being called 'nig-nog' or 'sambo' and would laugh along to Eddie Booth deriding his neighbour. After watching week-by-week it became apparent that it was the women who held the family reins. By the end of each episode the 'race' problem was always resolved and Bill Reynolds, played by Rudolph Walker, often got the upper hand over his white neighbours. We understood it was a comedy and we saw the funny side. Similarly, I didn't realise *The Black and White Minstrel Show* was racist until I was older and people started saying it was wrong for white actors to black-up their faces and dance.

A big television moment was when Lenny Henry won *New Faces* in 1975. I was so proud for him. Lenny came from a poor working-class background in Dudley and had the talent to make people laugh. The Beat recorded the backing tracks for his debut double-sided single 'The (Algernon Wants To Say) Okay Song' and 'Mole In The Hole', which was released in March 1981. 'The Okay Song' was co-written by the production team John Astley and Phil Chapman and was a

22

favourite on the Saturday morning kids show *Tiswas*. Lenny was an occasional contributor on the programme and he would get hundreds of letters a week asking him to perform the song.

Lenny moved on to be one of the presenters on the late-night ITV programme *OTT* and we met up when The Beat performed on the final episode in April 1982. We played 'Save It For Later', and then, during 'Stand Down Margaret', Lenny jumped on stage and started doing all his funny dancing in these ridiculous trousers with one leg red and the other green. Whilst Lenny was prancing about the other three presenters, Chris Tarrant, Bob Carolgees and Helen Atkinson-Wood were being hoisted up by pulleys above the audience. They sprayed champagne over everybody as hundreds of balloons were released across the stage and the studio floor. Lenny was totally anti-Margaret Thatcher, and after the show he said to the band, 'Good on you.' Lenny was an inspiration to all black kids. You rarely, if ever, saw black role models on television. Years later, people would say me and Pauline Black and Rhoda from The Bodysnatchers represented a sea change and through the 2 Tone movement put black people onto television screens and on the front page of newspapers and magazines. But for me, Lenny was the first.

At school, I had a reputation for being cheeky. I would get distracted by other kids, which set me off, and I would enjoy making the whole class laugh. I was a person of my own mind. I would answer teachers back if I thought I was in the right, stand my ground and tell them why. They didn't like it. 'Right, out,' or it was, 'Stand in the corner, Charley.' Teachers could get away with a lot more than they can today. I frequently used to get my hand slapped or have my ears pulled or be poked in the chest, which I hated. I often deserved it but I would feel my temper bubbling up. By the time I was thirteen, I would say to myself, 'Any minute now, I'm going to turn round and box you.' But also I would reason with myself, and say, 'That's not the right way. That's not the way to do it.' One time, there was a group of us throwing stones at the school building and I smashed a window in the cookery room. It was a perfect shot. A teacher confronted me, and said, 'Was it you, Charley?' I said, 'Yes.' I was marched to the head's office. I thought I was going to get expelled but I didn't even get suspended. That was down to Mr O'Sullivan, who was the Deputy Head.

A year earlier, I had written an essay that had turned Mr O'Sullivan and he became a kind of guardian angel who looked out for me. He should have expelled me about three times, but each time he gave me the benefit of the doubt. Racism in school wasn't exclusive to children. When we were taught about black history I remember one teacher said, 'If it wasn't for us lot you'd still be walking around in grass skirts and you wouldn't know how to use a knife and fork.' I was horrified. Nowadays, you could report that and the teacher would be sacked. After that, I started really studying. My sisters had studied black history, looking back to Ethiopia and the Egyptians, and I was receiving all this knowledge from them.

It was like, 'Bloody hell! Look what we've had to put up with. It's thousands of years old. They've tried to deny our history as if we've just appeared here out of the blue.' I wrote an essay about black history; about slavery and how black people had been treated and how it should have been equal and shared out. It was fifteen or twenty pages of heartfelt indignation. Mr O'Sullivan read it, and said, 'Are you sure you wrote this?' I said, 'Of course I wrote it! Some of the ideas have come from books but it's what I've read and studied and learnt.' He was the only teacher who ever saw anything in me. All the boys in the school hated him because they thought he was strict. But he liked me.

I was intelligent but I never did my homework. I couldn't be bothered. I was really good at English; spelling, reading and writing. I used to love home economics. My ideal job would have been carpentry. I was good at woodwork and science, but I was terrible at maths. I was a bit of a wild card. Teachers would say to me, 'You're going to end up sweeping the streets. You'll never get a job. You'll never get on in life. You're finished.' It was all doom, doom, doom. They wanted me to think I was a failure. I used to think, 'What kind of lives did they have?' I was out every night learning new things. They would say, 'We're not putting you in for your exams because you've been playing truant,' or, 'You're not trying hard enough,' or, 'You're too cheeky,' or, 'Make sure you wear your blazer tomorrow.' I would lie and say, 'My mum can't afford it.'

The exceptions were Mr O'Sullivan and my English teacher, the Girls Deputy Head Mistress, Mrs Sinecola. Whenever I got into trouble and had to stand outside the headmaster's office, she would give me a sweet, and say, 'Now, what are you in for this time, Roger? What have you done?' She would tell me how cute I was. She never cussed me. I got away with murder because I would always smile knowing it would thaw the ice. I'm still a smiler. A smile cuts across and gets to people. It's genuine. I was brought up to be thankful. 'You're here. You're alive. You're healthy.' That's the main thing. It's not about wealth. It's about maintaining your health and keeping a good head.

Mr O'Sullivan read all my schoolwork. He knew my story. He got me in his office, and said, 'There's something magical about you, Roger. You're a great charmer. You make everybody laugh. I've been your teacher now for three years. I've watched you from the beginning. You're better than that. Come on. Shape up. We want you to do well. This school's got a reputation, but I'm going to put you in for your English exams and you're going to do well at it.' Eventually, I told him I wasn't interested in qualifications and that they didn't mean anything to me. I told him, 'I'm interested in being a musician or an actor.' I knew I could hold an audience's attention and entertain people. That's how it all started. I thought, 'I could be anything.' I couldn't see how qualifications could help you become a successful musician. I didn't want to know about Beethoven or Stravinsky. In many ways, I had a great opportunity and I let it go. Oddly enough, in my late teens I began to listen to classical music, and *The Rite Of Spring* is one of my favourite pieces of music. Stravinsky was like the Sex Pistols of classical music. Be it a composer or Johnny Rotten, they were all rebels in their own way. That's why their music has stood out, because they had something different about them.

After 'Hands Off…She's Mine' was a hit for The Beat in 1980, I went back to Archbishop Williams to prove a point to the teachers who promised me I would end up sweeping the streets and to be brutally honest were fucking racists, as far as I was concerned. I'm now in my fifties and when I think about the way that they treated me, they gave me little to no hope. Revisiting the school wasn't planned. I had recently bought my first car, a Mini 1100, and I just turned up on a whim. I drove straight into the staff car park and then brazenly walked up the school drive. Before I reached the front foyer, kids started to recognise me and kids in the lower years were shouting, 'It's Charlery!' Within minutes there was all this commotion and I was mobbed. Mr O'Sullivan came out to see what all the noise was about, saw me, and shook my hand. I was invited into the headmaster's office: 'Would you like a cup of tea, Roger?' After, I met some of my former teachers in the staff room. Everybody shook my hand but I held my tongue. Surprisingly, the teachers who had hated me were the most friendly and grovelling. I didn't like that at all. I said, 'Is it all right if I walk round the school?' Very soon I was mobbed again. I thought,

'That's good enough. Job done. I can go now.' It was my way of saying to the kids, 'Look what is possible.'

* * *

When I was thirteen, I said to myself, 'One day I will be famous and I will be called Ranking Roger.' It was my nickname at school. This belief came from having the most profound dream: I could see this small circular room and all around people were standing up and clapping and I could see myself bowing. I couldn't see my face but I knew it was me. I woke up and I knew that was the way I must go. I said to myself, 'I'm going to be an entertainer.' The dream had an acute impact on my behaviour. I lost interest in school and fell in love with music and sound systems and musicians. I felt like a sponge and I knew that one day I would use everything I was absorbing and do it myself. By then I was in the fourth year, and instead of the proper uniform, I wore a military jacket to school with 'Ranking Roger Peace Love and Unity' written on it with a Star of David underneath the lettering. 'Peace, love and unity' became my mantra in life. I adapted the phrase from reggae musicians like Tapper Zukie and Big Youth, who would say things like, 'We all have to get on; black or white.' The idea imbedded in me. As a message, 'Peace, Love and Unity' says it all. It can change the world.

As school began to lose its appeal I found new avenues of adventure and pleasure hanging out with a gang of lads. There were about thirty of us. Typically, I would come home from school, change out of my uniform, do my chores, and then spend the evening out with friends, invariably playing football – or as I call it, 'bag of wind'. In later years, football became a focus of The Beat, and we formed a band five-a-side team. The first competition I can remember was when we played against a Radio 1 DJ team at Birmingham City's ground. The teams were made up of pop stars and actors. Of those involved I can remember Jasper Carrott, John Peel and Angela Bruce, the black nurse from the television series *Angels*. It was typical five-a-side football with end-to-end goals resulting in a 10-10 draw.

Another time, The Beat played at Loftus Road, the home of Queens Park Rangers, in a charity tournament. In advance of the tournament we trained in Handsworth Park. On the day, each team was allowed to field one professional player, and Tony Rance, the club secretary at West Bromwich Albion, assisted us. He also provided us with a complete strip. In all, twelve teams competed and several thousand people turned out to watch on a warm sunny afternoon. Unfortunately we didn't have much success on the pitch. In the first game The Fun Boy Three beat us 2-1. Gary Thompson, the Coventry and England under twenty-one striker, made mincemeat of our drummer, Everett, in defence. Dave Wakeling scored our only goal, but our bass player, David, who was tricky and persistent, went into a heavy tackle with Neville Staple and came out the worse, injuring his knee. As a replacement we roped in David's brother, Mick, who claimed to have played for the Isle of Wight. He scored in the second game against Coast To Coast, who had QPR's Ian Stewart playing for them. Andy Cox was in goal and made some memorable saves. I had no luck up front and the match ended a draw. The tournament was won by a side put together by the record producer Mickie Most. Despite our disappointment at being knocked out so early in the competition we were consoled by the fact that we had at least scored some goals – Madness didn't hit the back of the net all afternoon! Soon after we organised a friendly match on Primrose Hill with some friends from Telford and a couple of Beat Club members and won 10-1. Egos restored, I seem to remember we also played against Bow Wow Wow during an American tour in a hotel car park – the score was – to paraphrase the band's debut single – C·30, C·60, C·90 GO-AL!

Meantime, back in my school days, I had mates from all over the place – black, white, Indian – and we would hang out down the park until about eight or nine o'clock at night playing football or having mock black versus white fights. There wasn't any punching. We would just wrestle or try and get somebody in a headlock. You had the Stechford gang and the Yardley gang. These were kids between the ages of twelve and seventeen. It wasn't like gangs today. It was just a bunch of kids with nothing to do. It was like pretending to be in a gang. The Yardley side was mainly white and a lot tougher than us lot. Racist comments came more from them and you would get chased, but if you knew someone they would let you go. It was a laugh. Nobody got hurt. You'd be called 'wog' a lot.

In fact, there was a black guy from the Meadway called Gary. He was a good fighter so people didn't mess with him, but the white guys called him 'Woghead' and he just put up with it. Over time I developed my own ways of dealing with racism. If somebody said, 'You're a wog,' I would say, 'Yes, I am a Western Oriental Gentleman.' If they said, 'You're a nigger,' I'd say, 'That's one of the longest rivers in the world,' with the knowledge that the word derives from the River Niger where slaves were exported from West Africa. I would use my mouth but non-aggressively. I was trying to teach them something. Of course, if all else failed I punched them.

I didn't go out looking for trouble but if a fight came my way I knew how to defend myself. On the rare occasions when I did react, I would punch hard and let my feelings be known: 'Don't you say that again. Who are you talking to like that?' Occasionally a knife might have been used, but I never carried a weapon. In the end many of our gang decided we had to defend ourselves properly and we learnt martial arts and boxing. Soon after two of my cousins were attacked by a gang of racists in the Bull Ring. They were badly bruised but their martial-arts training saved them. You had to learn self-defence. It was a must to protect yourself. Stechford was quite rough but a fight is just a fight. Once it's done everyone shakes hands and it's over. There was a lot of racism but more people were anti-racist. The casual violence can be overplayed; in general white and black kids mixed. And if we weren't playing football together it would be cricket.

31

'Sticks and stones will break my bones but names will never hurt me' was drilled into me as a child, but they do. Thankfully, the Charlerys were outgoing and got on with people. There's been many a time when I've got on with racist people. When I've asked them why they're racist they don't really know. I concluded their bigotry came from their parents. I would say, 'If you like me you can't be racist.' They would say, 'You're all right, Roger. It's the others.' I would say, 'I am the others. I'm a representative of the others.' 'No, but you're different.' I've walked through life not making an issue of what colour I am. I don't look in the mirror every day and see a black man. To me, I'm a human being. I'm a person walking the planet. I don't see black, I don't see white, so why should I see it in other people? I may be aware of how many black people are in a room or how many white people, but it doesn't mean anything, until there's trouble. Then it may mean something.

I was a defender not a fighter. I remember being fifteen and going to the Bull Ring Centre and seeing a black guy about to beat up a white guy. I stepped right between them and said, 'Whoa! I want peace, love and unity in the place, man. We don't want no war.' I broke the whole thing down. This other black guy came up to me and said, 'Hey brother. You're not to do that. That guy might have had a knife. He might have stabbed you.' I said, 'No. This is what I stand for.' If you caught me in the right mood I would be the most help to anybody. If I liked you I would do anything for you. But there was a side to me that was just rebellious. I'd do things and not think about them. Later on, I'd think, 'That was pretty stupid.' One time the police caught my mates and me filling up condoms with water and throwing them at passing buses on Bordesley Green East. Fortunately we were let off with a warning. Another time, I threw a stone and it smashed the side window of the bus. How I got away with it I'll never know. But then I did have a run-in with the police and I wasn't so lucky.

I knew this Irish guy called Brendan who lived on our road and had a motorbike, which he'd made out of odd parts from other bikes. We were riding the bike up and down Stuarts Road; it was a quiet area so I ventured a little further. Halfway round the block I was stopped by a policewoman driving to work. She got out of the car and grabbed my hand, and said, 'You're not going anywhere.' I was trying to twist my hand out of her lock and accidentally I let go of the bike and it fell on her leg. I screamed, 'Oh my God,' and I started running towards the park. There was a narrow clearway and I ran straight into a policeman. He tried to rugby tackle me but I jumped up just in time and carried on running. The River Cole runs through Bordesley Green East and I somehow managed to get across it to the other side, where there was a community hall with a local event happening. I slipped in. I could hear sirens wailing all around. I sat down in a corner trying to catch my breath and fortunately nobody paid me any attention. I must have stayed seated for about two hours and then I cautiously walked home. A week later two policemen came to the house. Mum opened the door and said, 'What's he done?' They said, 'Your son has stolen a motorbike.' I was protesting and Mum just said, 'All right. Take him.' They handcuffed me on the doorstep and put me in a police panda car. It was rush hour and I remember looking out of the window at the passengers on the buses on the main road and feeling ashamed. It was the first time I had ever been arrested. I was driven to the police station, where they took my fingerprints and put me in a cell. I was left for a few hours but every so often someone would come to the cell and try and intimidate me: 'It's really bad what you've done. That's one of our own you've hurt.' It was a tactic to make me feel small. It worked. I remember crying and feeling like it was the end of the world, and thinking, 'Am I going to end up in prison?' Eventually I was released and I went home. It was all brimstone and fire: 'Shame on the family. I didn't bring you up for you to bring police to my doorstep.' I got beaten with a stick – on my arm, my legs, on my back – and I had to stand there and take it.

The case went to court and I was given two years' probation for assaulting a police officer, because the motorbike had fallen on her leg. My probation officer, John Barnard, said, 'The injury to the police officer was not intentional. The boy panicked. Roger is as good as gold.' The case for theft was dismissed. John used to drive around in a black cab and take all of the kids he looked after on rehabilitation trips: camping and stuff like that. He lived on a barge behind Winson Green prison. I did everything he told me to do. I stayed on his boat one night and he had a coal fire. It was brilliant. In the morning, he said, 'I've been seeing you for three months now, Roger. There's nothing wrong with you. I don't want to see you again'. In a way, I think he grew to love me. He was there to deal with problem boys and just saw me as a good kid wasting his time. I wasn't a serious troublemaker.

I never sat an exam. I left school at fifteen and they didn't see me again. At home, Mum couldn't control me either. She thought I was rude and wanted me out of the house. She would say things like, 'I've tried and I've tried and you don't listen to me. You're unruly and do your own thing. You'll only learn when you get in trouble with the police.' All my sisters left home one by one when they were sixteen and I followed in their footsteps. The day I turned sixteen – February 22, 1979 – I left school, left home and found myself living in a hostel. I had been brainwashed by the punks and the Rastas who I had begun to hang out with in town. They would talk about how the system was a fraud and that there was one law for the poor and another for the establishment. I thought, 'Stuff the system. I want to do it my way. I'll be part of the underground and the working class.' I was in a state of confusion. I didn't know what to believe in. There was so much propaganda out there. Unemployment had risen to over a million and a half. There was an Iron Curtain across Europe. And there was a growing fear of nuclear war. People speculated about the realistic possibility of a Third World War. On television they were showing public information programmes about what to do in the event of a nuclear attack. It heightened the fear in my generation of nuclear annihilation.

Coupled with the troubling and escalating political uncertainty was an ever-present boredom. Most of the kids I knew from school ended up working in shops and factories or turned to theft. Nobody got into sport or music. The careers advice I had been given was meaningless and offered nothing I could relate to. School was a process, but not a learning process. I was determined not to stay in Stechford and go down the drain like everybody else I could see around me. Although, in my state of confusion, I briefly got a job as an apprentice car mechanic. It is the only proper job I have ever had. I had to unscrew vehicle parts and learn about brake fluid and how to change an oil filter. It was small, menial work. After a week I realised it wasn't for me and left. I didn't want to be under a car all day covered in oil. A lot of the punks I was hanging out with lived in squats and like them I couldn't imagine buying or renting a house, with brown envelopes coming through the door for the rest of my life and somebody always asking me for money, so I got a room in a hostel for young offenders organised by my probation officer. The rent was covered by Social Security but when the cheque was delivered I pocketed it. The Shape Trust was on Cattell Road opposite the Birmingham City ground in Small Heath. In my room I had a bed and a table, a portable radio and some clothes I'd taken from home. That was it. I was poor so I didn't have many possessions. There was a communal kitchen with basic cooking facilities and I somehow found food, or friends would cook for me. It wasn't uncommon for people to have their belongings stolen but in general I didn't worry about the dangers of living in a hostel. There was a lock on my door but I knew it would be easy to kick down if somebody wanted to break in. The hostel was manageable and I actually felt lucky. I was sixteen. I hadn't officially finished school but for the first time in my life I was in the big wide world. I remember laying my head down on the bed and thinking, 'What am I going to be doing tomorrow with the punks? I'm sixteen and I'm old enough to do what I want.' It was an exciting time. I didn't care about money. All I needed was a weekly giro. I signed on and got the social to pay my rent, but in hindsight, if The Beat hadn't happened I would probably have ended up working in a factory like everybody else did from school.

Do You Really Want To Hurt Me?

Punk. Sound systems

I can't remember how I ended up going down the Crown – a punk hang-out on Hill Street opposite New Street Station in the late Seventies – but from the first time I stepped through the door I was made welcome. I was fifteen and still at school. My hair was short and spiky and I had a leather jacket and bondage trousers. I was scruffy. Later, when I started wearing punk clothes they were like, 'Oh, you're one of us.' The first thing I did was rip a Union Jack flag, to signify a broken down country, and put it through the D-ring on my bondage trousers. I also attempted to dye my hair. It came out ginger. I would have to do it twice to make it blonde and then I could put in other colours. I knew this punk girl called Lesley from the Crown who worked in the Kahn and Bell boutique and she dyed my hair red, yellow and green using something with a vegetable substance.

Fashion was what it was all about. Steve Gibbons, of the Seventies rock band The Steve Gibbons Band, was married to the designer Patti Bell, who with Jane Kahn owned Kahn and Bell. Patti and Jane used to make punk clothes; they would buy trousers and tops from thrift shops and sew zips and bits of bondage into them. Every item was an original. Kahn and Bell was on Hurst Street in the city centre. Before their shop opened, if you wanted to buy punk clothes you had to go to London. Now, people travelled from all over to buy clothes from Kahn and Bell. When I could afford it I would buy clothes from Patti and think nothing of ripping a pair of trousers or slicing them with a knife.

Across town, George O'Dowd, and his friend Martin Degville – who would later join Sigue Sigue Sputnik – ran a clothes stall in Oasis, an indoor clothes market, called Dispensary. George and Martin always dressed extravagantly and would happily wear dresses and make-up. One day they would dress as women and the next they would be wearing baggy calottes, which looked dangerously like clown trousers. They were totally different. They weren't punks but they'd mingle in with the scene. When Culture Club broke in the early Eighties with 'Do You Really Want To Hurt Me?' the country was shocked to see George dressed as a woman, but it was old news to us. You had poseurs pouting but anything weird went with punk. It was a community which encompassed everybody. You could be male, female, black, white or gay. As long as you were poor or working class you were in. You were part of the clan. We weren't looking out for them, but we were always suspicious of middle-class punks pleading poverty. You could tell them apart by speech, or more easily when squatters were evicted by who went home and who ended up on the street; the rich kids always went back to Mummy and Daddy to have a shower and be fed. That said, although some punks came from rich families they genuinely didn't want their parents' lives, and rejected their privileged backgrounds to make their own way. More often than not, if you were a punk you were the black sheep of your family.

Even though punk was big in the national media there weren't that many punks, and certainly being a black punk in Birmingham was a novelty. I was an eye magnet. I'd go into town on the bus and get comments: 'A black punk!' I enjoyed it. I've always had the mindset 'dare to be different... don't be like the rest... walk your own walk'. The more I hung around with the punk crowd, learning about them, the more I liked what I saw. Regardless of people's often negative opinions of punks, in Birmingham they treated all races the same. Black and white mixed; everyone was equal. It was a great thing. It was a coming together of disaffected teenagers with an attitude of 'we look after our own'. If you were in trouble you were looked after. Many punks had the kindest hearts I'd ever encountered. To look at them you might think, 'My God, I wouldn't like to bump into you down a dark alley.' I would hear racist remarks sometimes but my friends would back me up. I would say, 'You can call me a black bastard, but there's one of you and seven people here ready to have a go at you.' There was that sense of community. I felt lucky to be amongst them. Black people would say to me, 'What are you doing? Don't you know your culture and your history?' I would just walk on and do my own thing.

It was a shame that a lot of those people got into alcohol dependency or glue sniffing or harder drugs, like cocaine and heroin. It took many a life. I managed to keep away from all of that. The first time I went to the Crown I met a guy called Graham, who would later die of a heroin overdose, and he gave me a tablet. I looked at it, and he said, 'Go on, take it.' I pretended to swallow it. I found out later it was a blue. All the punks used to take speed. 'Oh! That's why they're up all night doing that wide-eyed business!'

One of the main attractions of the Crown was its jukebox and its fantastic selection of punk records. 'New Rose' by The Damned was always played. Generation X. Early Adam & The Ants. These songs became our fashion and our movement. I would argue with the punks because they also listened to 'Heroes' and 'Space Oddity'. I would say, 'David Bowie isn't punk so why are you listening to him.' 'No, no, no, Roge. We got our fashion from Bowie and Iggy Pop. That's why we dress the way we do.' The band that really got me into the whole scene was Devo, who were a weird American band. I bought their album *Are We Not Men? We Are Devo!* Were they electronic? Were they punk? It was experimental. It was great.

There were also a couple of commercial reggae tracks on the jukebox, like 'Uptown Top Ranking' by Althea & Donna or 'Dat' by Pluto. Generally speaking, British reggae didn't appeal to me. I saw bands like Aswad and Misty In Roots as part of a universal Jamaican sound. It was only with 2 Tone that reggae truly became British. Whereas Steel Pulse and Aswad were trying to be like the Jamaicans, we weren't. 'Mirror In The Bathroom', for example, was British black reggae. It had Jamaican strains but it was born in England. They were singing about 'Jah' and Rastafari while we were still singing about peace and love and warning people about the establishment. Rasta would say 'don't trust Babylon' and I would say 'don't trust the system'. Our lyrics were all about being aware, take warning, don't trust, see what's coming round the corner. There were natural similarities but The Beat spoke in an English way.

All that said, I was a massive fan of *Handsworth Revolution* by Steel Pulse. It was conscious lyrics but it was the music that caught me. It was so different to anything else I had heard. It had such a unique vibe. My sister, Equilar, has been friends with the band's singer, David Hinds, since they were young and she has been passing messages between us for the past thirty years. Whenever I went to clubs or parties or gigs I would see Selwyn, the keyboard player, and Grizzly, the drummer. Around 1990, Special Beat did a tour with Steel Pulse and Daddy Freddy, who was the fastest rapper in the world at the time. We mashed up the place. When we played on the East Coast all the black people came out. It was a Jamaican crowd. Sadly, they weren't impressed by me and Neville Staple jumping up and down to the up-tempo numbers and preferred the more relaxed reggae tracks like 'Spar Wid Me' and 'Doors Of Your Heart'.

I listened to the underground sound of reggae a lot, people like Burning Spear, Dennis Alcapone, Clint Eastwood, Dillinger, Big Youth, Trinity and Lee Perry. It may come as a surprise, but back then I wasn't a Bob Marley fan particularly. I respected what he said and stood for but to my mind Marley was the commercial side of reggae. It was like with the punks, once one of our bands got into the charts we didn't want to know any more: 'They've sold out!' Bob Marley once asked The Beat to open up for him at a gig in Dublin but we couldn't logistically do it because we were in America. I was like, 'Oh no! I'm a fan now!'

I remember hearing John Lydon on the radio talking about how punks should listen, not necessarily to the music, but to what the reggae artists were saying. He said, 'They're saying exactly the same thing as what we're saying. We're fighting the same struggle.' I thought, 'Whoa! That's put it right there.' Reggae was saying 'Chant Down Babylon' and punk 'Anarchy In The UK'. They shared the same attitudes about working-class people being in control, instead of the establishment. Lydon is rich now and lives in the United States. Fantastic! He did his job. He changed a generation and made people, like me, think differently. We might have all been bigots and greedy bastards if it wasn't for him.

* * *

Music was like a magnet. The first record I bought was 'Pick Up The Pieces' by the Average White Band when I was about eleven or twelve. I had saved up for it with paper-round money and then I played it to death. I loved the brass section and the funky guitars and the groove. For years, I thought they were an American band until I was told they were from Scotland. I would always be listening to Radio 1. One of favourite tunes was 'A Horse With No Name' by the rock band America. Songs like that would make me want to cry. I was influenced by so many different styles of music. In the early Seventies, when glam rock became the thing, I enjoyed Mud and songs like 'Ballroom Blitz' by The Sweet.

The first band I saw play live was in Dad's house. He lived on Stoney Lane in Sparkhill in an upstairs flat with his girlfriend, and downstairs in the basement a reggae band used to rehearse. I was about twelve and would sit in the room whenever they practised and study what they were doing. They used to play social clubs and small-time gigs, and played a mix of original songs and a few cover versions. They were all West Indians and must have all been in their thirties. They had a good drummer and the bass sound was heavy, but I didn't understand the music. It was too old for my taste. Nevertheless, it was my first introduction to musicianship and the flavour and feel of what it would be like to be in a band.

As I got older, I'd go to local gigs at places like the Star Club, the Red Star, and the Mermaid Pub on the Stratford

Road in Sparkbrook. The first big gig I saw was Big Youth in 1977, and then The Damned, The Skids and Dennis Brown soon after. I used to buy a lot of records from Don Christie Records – 'The Reggae Specialists: Steppers, Dubs, Calypso, Roots, Loversrock' – on the Ladypool Road, and then in the Rag Market when it opened a second shop in town. You would see a lot of guys from sound systems hanging round in there. There'd be a big line-up. Ezra, who was a big Rasta and worked behind the desk, would have six versions of one track; the same backing but by different artists. He would play about ten or fifteen seconds of the first record and anyone who wanted to buy it had to raise their hand, 'Yeah, I'll take one of them.' Then he'd put the next one on, 'No, leave that one.' I'd walk out with about three versions of the same tune. By the time I was earning in The Beat, I'd go to Don Christie's every couple of weeks and buy twelve or fifteen albums of reggae and dub, or a bit of soul or a Greensleeves Record. I would then go across to the reggae shop in Oasis or buy punk records from the small Virgin or HMV shops. I got the first French pressing of the Sex Pistols album with the title mistake '*Never Mind The Bollocks It's…*' instead of '*Here's… The Sex Pistols*'. 'Holidays In The Sun' was also misspelt as 'Holydays In The Sun' on the label.

From Mum's house, there was another black family who lived ten doors up from us, on the other side of the road. They had a son who was my age called Howard Hall – he was known as Double H – and he became my best friend.

45

We moved around together as teenagers. Howard was good for me and stayed out of trouble and avoided the attention of the police. Together, we learnt about sound systems and about black culture and our roots. We did a lot of things together and would often go to blues dances and sound system clashes. The first sound system I was involved in was called Ital Padel with some school friends. It wasn't very serious. We did a couple of dances. Howard and I also got involved with Magnum Hi-Fi. There were five of us. I used to control the mic and it had an echo chamber to give your voice effect. There was an art to dropping a seven-inch record; Jamaican records wouldn't have middles and there wasn't time to fix an adapter into the centre of a record because you had little more than a couple of seconds to switch discs while the MC announced the song title, so on the deck you would have to rest the knuckle on your finger against the middle spine on the record player. Normally you would have two or four fifteen-inch speakers, maybe a couple of mid-range speakers around seven inches, and some tweeters for treble. A 200-watt amp would be admired with two equalisers. We would do friendlies where each sound system would take it in turn and do an agreed time slot, maybe fifteen or thirty minutes. Each sound system would set up at opposite ends of the room and then, keeping an eye on the clock, you would try and win over the crowd. Nowadays people share the same PAs, but back then your own equipment could be the deciding factor.

We didn't do clashes. That was when you tried to bury the other sound system and send them packing. The winner was decided by audience response to your records and the noise they made. It is incredible that today sound system clashes draw crowds of more than 20,000 people. I started writing a futuristic sci-fi novel in the early 2000s. It's unfinished, but there was a chapter about a sound system clash. It was set in Digbeth and centred around two gangs, the ZoZos and the 20-20s. Simultaneously, a character from the University of Birmingham, who is researching energy in plants which can be transferred and used in car-manufacturing technology, becomes entangled with crime lords. The book has many hi-tech ideas, including a pack which enables you to see into the minds of other people. I hand-wrote in purple ink but I never finished it because work took over.

I was soaking up punk and reggae. I could see how they could both come together. Both genres' lyrics were rebellious. When Peter Tosh and Mick Jagger recorded '(You Gotta Walk) Don't Look Back' together it was two rebels linking together: The Wailers meets The Rolling Stones.

Then it becomes, 'Oh that was hip. Let's try it.' Later, Paul McCartney did 'Ebony And Ivory' with Stevie Wonder. They were just following fashion. McCartney – who I love and get to meet later in this book – and Wonder were the safe guys but the rebels always come first. Tosh was the rebel of reggae and Jagger was the rebel of rock. Jagger was doing his camp thing and Tosh was deadly cool. He had that look that said, 'Don't mess with me. I'm dangerous.' To this day, that's why I dress in black because it's mysterious and keeps people away.

(Clockwise from top) Frederick and Laura Augustin aka Pedro and Ma Pedro, my maternal grandparents; Dad and Mum's wedding, 1957; Equilar, Mum and me, circa 1964.

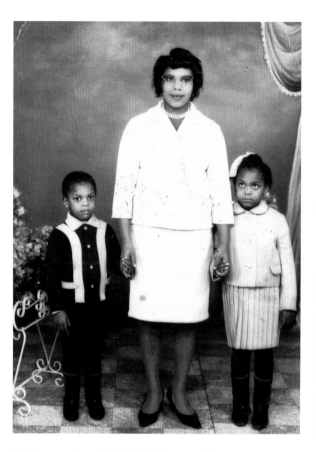

(Opposite, clockwise from top left)
me, Mum and Equilar, circa 1966;
me aged four, 1967; with Equilar
at our farewell party before
leaving for St Lucia, 1967; Annie,
Sandra, Mum, me and Equilar,
circa 1973.

(Above) outside home in
Stechford. Equilar, Merlinda
(niece), Mum and me, circa 1977.

(Clockwise from top, this page)
Record Mirror front cover, January 1980; practising at home, circa 1979; Dum Dum Boyz poster, supporting UB40 at Digbeth Civic Hall, April 28, 1979; poster for the gig where The Beat supported The Dum Dum Boyz, March 31, 1979.

(Right) outtake from *The Face* cover photoshoot, June 1981
© Sheila Rock

(Opposite above) Saxa in Germany, circa 1980; (below) Laurel Aitken with The Beat at the Lyceum, January 27, 1980 © *Virginia Turbett*.

(Above) me and Dave Wakeling, Belgium, May 2, 1980. © *Gie Knaeps/Getty*; (right) buried in sand, France, 1980.

(Above) **The Beat in concert at the Hammersmith Palais, London, June 1980** © *Andre Csillag/REX/ Shutterstock*; (left) **me and Everett Morton, 1981** © *Adrian Boot.*

Ire Feelings

Toasting. Rock Against Racism.
Dum Dum Boyz

Toasting is the same as MCing, or as Americans call it, 'rap'. It's a form of chanting. It originated in Jamaica when sound system operators like Prince Buster and Duke Reid would talk over records at dances making sounds like *hic, hic*. As reggae became more popular, people like Prince Jazzbo and Dennis Alcapone started to carry the swing; talking over backing tracks or reciting parts from The Bible. There was no definite style until toasters like Big Youth, Clint Eastwood, Trinity and Dillinger came to the fore. It coincided with twelve-inch records becoming more popular and the style developing from spoken word to being sung and half-spoken. In many ways it was like reading a nursery rhyme, where the last word of each line had to rhyme:

De sound a lead the way
Every hour every day
Don't get led astray,
But come what may.

Apart from Rupie Edwards, who had a Top 10 hit with 'Ire Feelings (Skanga)' in 1974, Neville Staple and I were probably the first two MCs to come forward from West Indian origin and have success. It had an impact because we were experimenting with pop music using Jamaican influences. In a way that was exactly what 2 Tone was all about.

I first used my voice when I was about nine. I was in the school choir for a short time but by secondary school didn't want to know. It had to be pop music; anything less than pop was classical, and that wasn't cool. Both Mum and my sisters could sing but it wasn't a big thing in the family. For me, it was MCing. Compared to straightforward singing I always thought it was harder because you had to put twice as many words in it. It meant you had to work harder at it, but it came naturally to me. I used to practise in my bedroom all the time, making up lyrics. I rewired a headphone as a microphone so I could hear it through my speakers. At first, I would use other people's lyrics and mix them with my own, like MCing over 'Good Times' by Chic, but mostly I practised over reggae records. The record that first inspired me to take up toasting was *African Dub All-Mighty Chapter 3* by Joe Gibbs & The Professionals, who were the rhythm

50

section Sly and Robbie. I used to toast over a dub on that record all the time.

I started copying MCs like Big Youth and I-Roy and U-Roy. I would hear all these fantastic records from my sisters at home or at blues dances and shebeens. People often ask what is a shebeen and is it different from a blues. They are the same thing. In Birmingham, shebeens often centred around Lime Grove in Balsall Heath in small terraced houses. They would be held in purpose-built sheds that could hold a hundred people. They would be smoky and cramped, with people dancing and drinking Red Stripe and liquor sold at an illegal pop-up bar. You had to pass yourself off as eighteen to be allowed in.

I kept practising MCing until I was fluent. One day, I performed a song by Ruddy Thomas called 'Loving Pauper' in front of the whole school and got a standing ovation. I thought, 'Bloody hell! Okay.' After that I would pick up the mic at school discos and MC. The other kids would go, 'Yeah! Go on, Roger.' At first the DJ wouldn't let me use his mic but I kept pursuing him. 'Go on, mate, just let me do a little eight bar, I'll show you.' Eventually my persistence wore him down. That gave me the confidence to hassle sound system operators outside of school and build my belief in what I wanted to do. I was self-propelled and determined. When there was a disco at the Crown I would grab the microphone and MC about the Sex Pistols and The Clash and people would say, 'He's all right, that black guy.' One night at the Crown, 'The Model' came on the jukebox – it was the closest Kraftwerk came to having a reggae bass line. If you listen to 'Love And Only Love' by Fred Locks it has an almost identical bass line, there's one note difference. I picked up the mic and MCed to it. Nobody had heard a toast over a rock record before.

The native tongue of St Lucia is Kweyol, which is like broken French, so I shouldn't sound like a Jamaican when I toast. In fact, there's no real connection between St Lucia and Jamaica. Geographically, there's over a thousand miles of sea between them; St Lucia is in the eastern Caribbean and is closer to Venezuela at the tip of South America. The majority of black people who I knew in England came from Jamaica, so that was my connection. All patois is a mixture of broken English, African and Creole. It was hip. I learnt the language from listening to records and from my friends and how my parents spoke at home. Basically from growing up around Jamaican people and from off the street. Nowadays I talk a combination of English, Yardie and street talk. I slip between all of them. I like being flexible. But thirty years ago a lot of people couldn't understand the accent. I'd go 'Wha'ppen?' and they'd go, 'What?'

I chose my nickname from school, 'Ranking Roger', to DJ. It had a natural ring with two 'R's and sounded more showmanship than an alternative like 'Jah Roger'. DJs would prefix their names with 'Jah' or 'Ranking'. There was Ranking Toyan and Ranking Joe. Ranking Dillinger was my hero. Joe Strummer referenced him in '(White Man) In Hammersmith Palais'. Dillinger had a tune called 'Marijuana In My Brain' in 1977, which I loved. It was psychedelic reggae. But then the following year he released 'Cocaine In My Brain', which I hated because I was anti-drugs. A lot of my style came from him. He had slogans like *No matter what the people say, these sounds, lead the way.* He took it from King Stitt's 'Fire Corner'. DJs borrowed words from each other all the time.

Around 1978, I started going to Barbarella's nightclub on Cumberland Street in the city centre. It was the place to go at weekends to see live music. Mike Horseman would DJ in-between the punk and reggae bands and I used to get up during his set and MC. He used to play tunes like The Clash 'White Riot', Sham 69 'Borstal Breakout' and then 'MPLA' by Tapper Zukie, which fits smack-a-dom in the middle. And the punks and Rastas would be up and dancing. It was like rebels together. Mike was known as 'The Shoop' and was the cool DJ on the scene. He had the biggest selection of records I ever saw. I thought Dad had the biggest collection until I saw Mike's. The records lined all the walls in his living room in alphabetical order. Mike became my first manager and tried to get me involved with The Specials. He was good friends with Jerry Dammers who had started the band, and would of course establish 2 Tone Records the following year. A chance to MC over The Specials arose when they played in Cannon Hill Park. They were midway through 'Gangsters' and there was a stage invasion. I got on stage and as I was about to grab the microphone and do my little eight bars they stopped playing because a wall collapsed. I thought, 'Chaa!'

Jerry Dammers says the first time he saw me toasting was at Barbarella's, toasting over 'I'm An Upstart' by the Angelic Upstarts. At the end of the night a crowd of us went to Pollyanna's nightclub on Newhall Street but I was refused entry because of my colour. The Commission for Racial Equality had ordered Pollyanna's to stop its 'race bar' six months before but the owners had ignored it and there was a march through the city centre to blockade the club. Jerry stayed outside to chat with me and I told him about a band I had recently joined called The Dum Dum Boyz (more of whom later). He said he would come to our next gig, which was a Stop Racism in Clubs benefit at Digbeth Civic Hall with UB40. He came but we were terrible and played out of time.

The Specials played Barbarella's when they were still called The Coventry Automatics. The Clash were booked to play but hadn't turned up and all these skinheads seemed to come out of nowhere, and were shouting, 'Sieg Heil, Sieg Heil' and 'National Front'. It was getting heavy and the punks were booing. Then they started saying to me, 'You've got to say something to 'em Roge.' Mike put a record on and I picked up the mic and started toasting at them, in time with the music, 'Fuck-off, fuck-off de Na-tion-al Front. Fuck-off, fuck-off de Na-tion-al Front'. The crowd picked it up and it was the first time that I made a connection between influence and controlling a crowd with the power of a microphone. I would never have realised I was capable of doing that before. Next thing, there was a riot: people fighting and throwing bottles and anti-fascist punks attacking the National Front. Mike and I had to duck down behind the decks, which overlooked the left-hand side of the stage. Eventually it got quietened down and The Specials went on. It was a tense gig. After that I decided that I was going to do everything within my power to put a stop to racism.

I first heard about Rock Against Racism through the punks at the Crown. They would talk about marches against racism and pamphlets would be handed out. There would be chat in the pub: 'I can't meet on Saturday because I'm going to a demonstration.' 'What demonstration?' 'The National Front are marching through town. We're going to stop them.' 'What! Okay, we'll all come.' Suddenly, another ten or twenty people wanted to be involved. The movement grew by word of mouth and I was introduced to activists from the Socialist Workers Party. Digbeth Civic Hall put on the most regular Rock Against Racism gigs. It was a good opportunity for new bands to stand or fall by their own graces. The nights would start with a couple of punk bands and then end with a reggae act to balance the evening and tone down the punks. I jumped on stage once when Mosiah were playing and I started to MC; the crowd went mad. Because I wore bondage pants with a ripped Union Jack flag and had orange hair and spiky half dreadlocks I started to get a name around town. I would regularly go and see punk bands, like The Ruts and Sham 69, but I always ended up toasting. One time a friend dared me to jump on stage during a Skids gig. I climbed up on the stage, shouted 'Come on then!' at the singer, Richard Jobson, and then quickly dived back into the audience. He didn't know what to do!

I would read about Rock Against Racism in *NME* and hear about it on the punk scene but it was rare for black people to read the rock music press. Unless it was in a paper like *Black Echoes* there was little information getting through. You might see posters that said 'Stop racism' but by and large the communication was disjointed. Rock Against Racism was for everybody, but when I went to any event the majority of the audience was noticeably white. It always bothered me. This was a group of white people with good intentions trying to get justice for black people. I was like, 'Get your black ass out and come and support this. They're trying to help you and change things.' People were cocooned in their separate cultures and there was a lot of justifiable mistrust. Rock Against Racism was a fantastic idea but I wasn't heavily involved with them politically. The change would come with 2 Tone, and with it the first real evidence of black and white cultures mixing on the dance floor.

In early 1978, I joined a band called Unity. We were a kind of punky reggae trio but lacked power. I was the MC and played drums. We never came to anything beyond a few rehearsals. My first proper band, as I mentioned earlier, was The Dum Dum Boyz, named after David Bowie and Iggy Pop's song on *The Idiot*. We were raucous punk but rhythmic. We never recorded any songs and only played about four gigs. The band was made up of two singers, Mark White and Paul Headford, who looked like a dark-skinned David Bowie and would later tragically take his own life, Mick Parry on bass and Paul Harris, who was half Kashmiri, half Irish, on guitar. Mark contracted polio as a child and sang leaning on his crutches. In his twenties, he was killed in a hit and run accident on the Coventry Road, near Sheldon. Mark's affliction was not dissimilar to Ian Dury, who also caught polio when he was a young boy. I met Ian in later years when he played with The Blockheads in Birmingham. I went backstage and shook hands with him. I remember him saying that The Beat was one of his favourite bands. Ian was a warrior. 'Hit Me With Your Rhythm Stick' was like an unorthodox English disco rap. The rhythm section of Norman Watt-Roy on bass and Charlie Charles on drums was dazzling.

The Dum Dum Boyz met on the way to a punk all-dayer at Barbarella's, and were members of the Socialist Workers Party. I joined the band shortly after and played drums. We used to practise on the first floor above the Socialist Workers Bookshop next to Digbeth Civic Hall. The SWP gave us the space for free because we said we did Rock Against Racism gigs and because of the multiracial mix of the band: Asian, black, white. I've always been aware that although 2 Tone is often recognised as the movement that instigated multicultural bands – The Specials, The Selecter, The Bodysnatchers – in Birmingham the mixing of white and non-white musicians before the label was established was not uncommon.

The SWP were nice people but quite hardcore left of centre, and some of them were mixed up in an organisation called Flame. Their intention was to persuade the black community to vote Labour. I saw them as a British Black Panther movement. I went to a couple of meetings and everything was 'black this' and 'black that'. The people running it were so aggressive. It was too black and I didn't like it or its Stalinist tendencies. They tried to involve me. I was like, 'What! You can't have black power in England. Where do you get that? It'll never happen. Trust me.'

We could rehearse above the SWP bookshop at any time so I would regularly go there and bash the drums and try to teach myself how to play. Quite often the bass player would come down and we would jam together. I made my first drum kit by putting together bits and bobs. I would buy a cymbal on the cheap and someone would give me a snare drum. It was a minimal kit but enough to get a noise out of it and very much in the 'do it yourself' spirit of punk rock. Before joining The Dum Dum Boyz I practised rhythm and timing by slapping my thighs and knees with my hands, but sat behind a real drum kit I found it hard to keep up the momentum for a whole song. And the challenge to maintain the same vigour for seven or eight songs severely tested my levels of stamina. I soon realised it would be easier to just be out front with a microphone.

The first time I ever met The Beat was at a Dum Dum Boyz rehearsal in 1979. We had a gig booked at a pub called the

Matador in the Old Bull Ring, and Dave Wakeling found out about it through a mutual friend in Oasis market. He contacted us, and said, 'Can we open up for you?' We said, 'All right, but you have to come and play some tunes for us first and if we like you we'll let you do the gig.' They agreed and came to our rehearsal room with their guitars. It's hard to explain my first impression of them: I thought that the singer was an alien and that the others were from another planet. I looked at their heads and their faces and their expressions and I thought, 'These guys are from somewhere else.' I remember Dave Wakeling had mascara on. I was a punk but it was the way they looked. It wasn't to do with their clothes so much as their faces. They were different. At that stage they were a four-piece – Dave, Andy Cox, David Steele and Everett Morton on drums. It wasn't unusual to see a black guy with three white guys – after all, The Dum Dum Boyz were a mixed-race band – but what was unusual was the sound of the music they made.

We played them a few tunes and they were like, 'Yeah, not bad.' Then they plugged into our amps, which were crap but were workable, and began to play. They started with a loose version of 'Mirror In The Bathroom', which they said they were still working on, but I thought, 'I like this – the bass player's heavy.' Then they played 'Twist And Crawl', 'Best Friend' and 'Save It For Later'. I was like, 'Fuck me! We don't stand a chance; we better play our hardest next week.' There was definitely a wow factor. The mix of punk bass and reggae drums was unlike anything I had heard before. It was neither punk nor reggae. I was totally taken aback by the deepness of the sound: the thud of the bass drum and the quirky bass lines. I definitely got that before the guitars. We shook on it, and said, 'You can do the gig. See you next week.' After they left, I sat behind the drum kit and both my snare and my kick drum had pock marks in them. I thought, 'That guy can hit 'em hard!'

We advertised the gig at the Matador on A4 white paper. It read: 'Rebel Social. Saturday 31 March. 8pm till late with DUM DUM BOYZ. Plus disco-bar. Tickets 60p. On The DOOR 75p. Reggae, rock, new wave.' The Beat weren't mentioned because they had only decided on the name of their band two days before. Years later, Dave explained to me how he came up with the name 'The Beat'. By looking up 'music' in a *Roget's Thesaurus* he found the word 'clash', which it said was 'to beat two things together'. It was very clever. Then he looked in the antonyms and under 'harmony' it said 'beat'.

The Matador was the debut gig for both bands, and mainly due to the fact that the rest of The Dum Dum Boyz used to drink there, the pub was rammed. The newly named Beat went on first. They played a short twenty-minute set and blew us off stage. Simply: they were great and we were awful. Soon after I went to see The Beat play at the New Inn on Moseley Road in Balsall Heath; they were supporting the Au Pairs who The Dum Dum Boyz had played an anti-sexism gig with. If you were anyone you played the New Inn and the Fighting Cocks. The Beat were playing 'Rough Rider' and I suddenly had an urgent desire to want to toast with them. I think Dave must have been able to see it in my eyes, because he signalled to me and I was up there in a flash. That was my first time performing with The Beat. And something happened on stage: the way Dave sang and I answered back… it worked.

A fortnight later, The Beat began an eight-week residency at the Mercat Cross on Bradford Street, behind Digbeth Coach Station, and they invited me down. The Mercat was a horrible modern-looking building. The live room was an oblong-shaped room with shabby tables and worn chairs, accessed up a narrow flight of stairs. There was a bar on the right-hand side and the stage area lay flat on the left. At a push the room could probably hold up to two hundred people. I got down an hour early and I was talking to Dave. He said 'There's nobody here. I don't know what to do.' It was free to get in but they needed the bar tabs. I said, 'Give us half an hour.' He said, 'You are coming back to toast with us, aren't you?' I said, 'I'll be back.' I went up to the Crown, where it was full of my punk friends, and I said, 'Hey! You know the band who opened up for us at the Matador? They're playing at the Mercat. It's free to get in.' It was a Tuesday night, nothing was happening and all these punks were bored out of their minds. So about fifty or sixty of them agreed to come back with me. We all left together and as we walked through town we looked a massive gang. They were all poking me, and going, 'You better be right, Roger. It better be The Beat.' Suddenly, a white police van slowed down and drove alongside us. We must have looked really suspicious. Fortunately they didn't do any more than just stare at us and then drove on. By the time we got to the Mercat the place was heaving. The band couldn't believe it and during the gig I was pushed onto the stage: 'Go on, Roger. Do your thing.' I toasted on a couple of numbers, sharing Dave's mic, and then stepped off stage again only for the crowd to shove me back on. At the end of the night, the band were all thanking me, and saying, 'You were really good.'

The Beat laid their foundation at the Mercat. I went down every week. It was always full of people. Over the summer their set expanded and included 'Mirror In the Bathroom', 'Tears Of A Clown', 'Twist And Crawl', 'Best Friend' and covers of 'Jackpot' by The Pioneers and 'Conscious Man' by The Jolly Brothers. More often than not the punks would push me on stage, and say, 'Go on! Now!' And I'd get up and MC on 'Two Swords' or 'Click Click' or 'Rough Rider'. Dave would say, 'We're doing a gig at so-and-so, come and join us. Any time you want, Roge. Anywhere where you think there's a harmony. Come in. Come up and do one.' People would say, 'You lot could go far. You do punk and you do the reggae and it's mixed.' Their belief and support gave me the confidence to believe in myself, and think, 'I'm doing the right thing, then.'

It was around this time that I could have joined UB40. I remember getting up with them at the New Inn to do a tune and it brought the house down. Ali Campbell said in his book *Blood and Fire*, 'There's a brilliant piece of film of us performing with Ranking Roger. It looks straight out of the Cavern.' UB40 were from around Moseley and Balsall Heath and I would see Ali and Earl Falconer at blues dances. They came from the same stable. Their influence and sound – the filtering effects on the guitars and keyboards – was inspired directly from Lee Perry and Black Ark Studios. Earl played the heaviest bass I'd ever heard but I thought their music was too mellow for my toasting. It was like space-age reggae, whereas The Beat was more punk, which is what I liked, and they were more versatile and aggressive. UB40 and The Beat did a few gigs together before either band was signed. There was always friendly competition between us, but in the end I had to choose between them. During the summer, The Beat invited me to a meeting. I sat and listened, thinking, 'Things are looking good for them.' Then they said, 'We think we've found a new agent. He's called John Mostyn. He books gigs for The Specials.' Everything was looking really positive. And then at the end they said to me:

'You've been quiet. Is there anything you want to say?'

'What! Me? I'm just listening.'

'No, no, no, say something if you've got something to say.'

'Well, I've been hanging around with you guys for a while. I want to know if I'm in or if I'm out?'

'It's obvious, you're in or you wouldn't be here.'

There was a big roar of laughter and comments like, 'Ah, stupid question!' 'Come on, of course, you're in.'

That was it. I became the fifth member of The Beat.

Shake Some Action

**The Beat. Life in Moseley. The Selecter.
John Peel Session**

O ver time, I have pieced together how the original four members of The Beat met and formed the band. This is the story, as I know it. In November 1977, Dave Wakeling and Andy Cox moved to the Isle of Wight to work for Andy's brother-in-law building huge wooden solar panel frames fitted with steel girders. They lived in a clifftop cottage close to the Blackgang Chine theme park, and it was there that Andy taught Dave how to play guitar. Dave was left-handed and played the guitar upside down. They put an advert in the local paper, *County Press*, which read, 'Bass player needed to form a group with original songs to shake some action'. The only person to respond was a reggae fan called David Steele. The three of them hit it off, and after writing a few songs together they all relocated to Birmingham in September 1978.

While David was training as a psychiatric nurse at All Saints' Hospital, near Winson Green, he asked a work colleague if she knew any drummers and was introduced to her friend's boyfriend. Everett Morton was born in St Kitts and moved to England when he was fifteen. At some point he had played drums with Joan Armatrading and had recently left a local band called Soul Of Man. Everett went to listen to some songs at Dave's flat and then agreed to join them at the Yorkshire Grey on Dudley Road for a rehearsal on a Tuesday evening. Apparently it took a while for Everett to be convinced he was the right man for the job, but once they connected, he joined the band and they began to merge punk and reggae as a basis for their sound.

When I joined the following year, The Beat were not only a quintet but five unique individuals from totally different backgrounds. Andy and Dave had been to college. David was a trainee nurse and Everett worked in a kettle factory. I would talk to Dave about black culture and he would explain the politics of the music business: what made the industry work; and who was running it. In later years, when we negotiated contracts, he would explain the terminology and nuances, and say, 'You know what that means, Roge? They've got you by the balls. Watch. We're going to get rid of that clause.' I was like, 'Wow! This is serious. I better pay attention.' Dave was a great teacher and opened my awareness to the loopholes in the business. Andy was a quiet, humble bloke and very balanced. He said the least but when he did speak he was worth listening to. I could never wrong him and he never said anything untoward to anybody. I never knew him to be arrogant or forceful or vicious but if you upset him he would let you know. David was very intelligent. I always assumed he came from money but I never asked him if that was the case. I think one of his parents was a doctor but I never met them. His hair was quite curly and he had darkish skin, perhaps Mediterranean. He was quirky and I liked his ways.

As the band began to play gigs we all had to get to know one another. We met up and got on. It was natural. I went in and was myself. I watched and learnt. I trusted them all straight away and recognised them as genuine people. I will never forget the courtesy those guys gave me. They were so good to me. I was a cheeky little sixteen year old who had just left school, but I had a talent. I could grab the mic and make people smile and I could get a crowd going from nothing. I don't know where it came from but whenever I had to I could get up and do it.

Everyone was busking it. No one had any money. We would do the odd rehearsal at the New Inn or at Andy's house at 15 City Road, which he shared with his girlfriend Malu, who would later adopt the fictitious name Marilyn Hebrides and run The Beat fan club. We would all squeeze into the back room. It was very minimal. I don't think Andy had a TV. There were just a few cushions on the floor, no sofa, and a table to eat at. We didn't have a microphone or a PA so everybody had to play quietly to hear me and Dave singing. In rehearsal we would organise the structure of the songs. Dave was always very vocal and Andy was a great arranger with a natural sense for how things should fall into place. David too. There was a lot of smoking and talking and laughing. We would rehearse every couple of weeks and occasionally at Dave's sister's flat on Gough Road – one of the posh roads in Edgbaston – creating our own style from diverse influences such as Elvis Costello, The Velvet Underground, Lee Perry, Prince Buster, The Clash. We didn't try to copy anybody else, we just took the best from everything we liked and created our own music. The whole Beat journey was to be an adventure of not knowing musically what was going to come next.

Once we started to earn some money we got a rehearsal room above a motorbike shop on the Stratford Road, near the Birmingham City ground. You had to ring on a bell and someone would buzz you in from upstairs. It was a big square room on the first floor with a PA system in it and I remember it being freezing in there. All these schoolgirls found out we rehearsed there and would hang out on the street below trying to listen to our new tunes.

As the youngest member of The Beat – David was a couple of years older and Andy, Dave and Everett were all five years older – in the early days I had to lie about my date of birth, as you had to be eighteen or over to play in clubs. We made our first demo after saving up money from all the small gigs we'd been doing. We recorded in a cheap studio in Worcester, just outside of Birmingham, in a small room, recording four tracks including 'Jackpot' and 'Mirror In The Bathroom'. It was the first studio I had ever been in and I looked at the mixing desk with all the effects and faders and dials in awe. I was fascinated by the whole process of how the sound was controlled and how each instrument was isolated on a separate track. After a day's recording we emerged with a cassette tape. We played it to friends and anyone in our path. I'd say, 'Listen! I'm in a band called The Beat.' 'Oh yeah.' 'No, really, listen to this.' 'Bloody hell, that's good!'

We did a lot of gigs and started spreading our wings beyond Birmingham. We had a van and John Mostyn drove. I used to like sitting in the back amongst all the equipment. We were all really excited and there was a lot of laughter and cans of beer and sharing spliffs. They were great days full of anticipation and positive vibes. Despite being the new boy I was never left out, and if anything became the band joker. We were in a bubble of potential success. The first gig out of Birmingham was in Wales. When we got to the venue it was like a barn. It was exciting to play to strangers and as soon as we played 'Tears Of A Clown' we won the crowd over. There was a sense of achievement amongst us: we had booked the gig ourselves and people who didn't know us loved the music.

One night, after we'd all been out, Dave said to me, 'I'll give you a lift home.' Dave used to ride this motorbike, a ZX or something, and I would sit pillion. He took me back to the hostel and I said, 'Do you want to come in?' He came in, took one look around, and said, 'Roger, you're not staying here.

You're coming to live with me, mate. I'm not having you in this place. You're a good man. Come on.' I packed up my few possessions in a plastic carrier bag, slung it over my shoulder, and said goodbye to the hostel.

Moseley is small village four miles outside of the city centre but it's unlike anywhere else in Birmingham. For a start it has always been very multicultural. In the Seventies a lot of the hippies bought houses in and around the area, and as a result it has a very laid-back atmosphere: a mix of teachers and lawyers and students; a community melded into one. You never knew who you might meet at a party. I had always wanted to live in Moseley, and thought, 'This is going to be a good break for me.' I ended up living there for the next twenty years. Dave lived at 19 Park Road in a ground floor flat with a couple of spacious rooms. We went into the front, and Dave said, 'You have this as your room. You can sleep in here.' Dave had a big heart. He bailed me out and took me in and we got on great. He was very trustworthy but it was a cold flat and the bills were expensive. I was always hugging the heater. I used to wrap my head in a sheet around a small sun lamp. It used to make me feel like I was in the Caribbean.

I stopped going to the Crown as much and started to hang out with Dave and the others, which coincided with Barbarella's in the city centre closing down. Without an obvious alternative nightclub, the scene moved to people's houses and there would be at least three or four parties every weekend.

Moseley was the hot spot: Ali Campbell lived on the corner of Trafalgar Road, and the adjacent Kingswood, Sandford, Queenswood, and Anderton Park were all party roads. The Au Pairs lived up the road from Dave's flat and they used to have a lot of parties too. Dexys Midnight Runners used to come and cause bother. They were rough and liked to fight other musicians. David Steele ran into a couple of them one time in town and he said they were looking for trouble. Accusations of racism seemed to follow them around. Mickey Billingham, who ended up playing keyboards in General Public, used to tell me stories about Kevin Rowland. I was surprised because Kevin's complexion suggested he had darkness in his heritage. Mickey said the brass section used to take riffs from Aswad's 'Warrior Charge' and bits and pieces from old reggae tunes and subtly incorporate them in their parts. Kevin didn't know. I thought, 'That's fucking clever. I like that. Get their own back.'

The Au Pairs and The Beat played a lot of gigs together. Musically they were like cousins to the Gang Of Four, and would do a lot of Rock Against Racism gigs. Lesley Woods, the singer, especially, was really up for women's rights. Anything that was even slightly anti-women she would have a go at us for. When she took umbrage to our version of 'Whine And Grine', Dave plucked up the courage, and said, 'Well, don't people have sex?' I didn't hang out with the Au Pairs much but I'd see Pete, the drummer, at gigs and I got to know the guitar player, Paul, after they split up in the early Eighties. He got into jazz and played with Andy Hamilton for many years after. Moseley was full of new bands starting and splitting up. Everybody wanted to be in a band.

As a five-piece, we continued playing small places through the summer of 1979, and then we were offered a support with the recently formed Selecter at Cascade in Shrewsbury. Neol Davies and John Bradbury had recorded an instrumental track called 'The Selecter' on a four-track recording machine in Roger Lomas' shed at the end of his garden. Roger would go on to have a successful career producing records for the likes of The Selecter, The Bodysnatchers and Bad Manners. With added ska-styled guitar, at the request of Jerry Dammers, 'The Selecter' was issued on the reverse of the self-financed 'Gangsters' by The Specials. It was the first 2 Tone Records single. The label was the brainchild of Jerry and was named after the black-and-white sticker tape from his bicycle as a child. Although 2 Tone was established as an independent label and the first single was picked up by Rough Trade, Jerry signed a deal with Chrysalis Records to market and distribute future records. Part of the deal licensed 2 Tone to sign up to ten bands a year with a budget of £1,000 per record. Crucially, any band had the freedom to leave 2 Tone and sign to a new label at their discretion. I admired Jerry for starting 2 Tone. It was founded with a punk DIY spirit and built on socialist principles of fairness and equality.

Our first gig in Shropshire went great and during our set Neol Davies, Pauline Black and Charley Anderson from The

Selecter were dancing in the audience. Neol offered us more dates and said we could support The Selecter whenever we wanted to and they would pay our petrol money. I liked their band. The sound was hard and heavy and I got on with them. Pauline made an immediate impression. She could hold her own and I thought, 'I wouldn't mess with you.' I got on with her and saw her almost like an older sister, but a lot of people didn't. If you've got six guys in a band, and you're the only woman, you can imagine the sexism and how pushy they would be – 'I'm the man around here.' Not to mention the effects of drink and drugs within the band. Pauline wouldn't allow any nonsense. She was strict and as the lead singer she kept the boys in order and would put any one of them in their place. The late Seventies was a fantastic time for women in music but they still had to survive in a male dominated industry. It would have been the same, and as challenging for any one of Pauline's peers: Siouxsie Sioux, Poly Styrene, Chrissie Hynde or Debbie Harry.

I totally respected Pauline. Even today, if her band is out of order she puts them in their place. It's a strength of hers. She's a serious worker and she's a woman of her word. The Selecter and The Beat reunited and have been touring with each other since 2014. It has taken both bands all over the world: from a tumultuous night at the Roundhouse in Camden in 2018, filmed in front of 4,000 fans, to Europe, the United States, Australia and Japan. The thirst and love for our music four decades since we first did gigs together is quite incredible. The two bands work really well together and my relationship with Pauline is brilliant. When we hang out, we might talk about last night's show or just everyday trivia. On the road, I tend to hang out more with Gaps – who was also an original vocalist in The Selecter – as Pauline is more of a loner and likes her own space. If there was a problem I'd soon know about it. But to be honest, if she comes into our dressing room it's usually because The Selecter haven't got any milk.

During the summer months of 1979, we ended up doing five gigs with The Selecter. After playing around the Midlands, and then in Blackpool and Sheffield, we supported them in London at the Nashville Rooms in September. It was packed with about five hundred skinheads. From backstage we could see the audience shouting 'Sieg Heil' and doing Nazi salutes. We were all terrified. The atmosphere was more like a football match. I was like, 'I've got to go on stage to that? What's going to happen? The first coin that's thrown at me I'm down in that audience. I'll knock 'em out.' We went on and throughout the gig the chanting continued. I was saying to myself, 'Just keep going. If you jump into the audience someone might have a knife.' Thank God we were good and there wasn't any serious trouble. The flagrant Nazism on show was a shock but we went down really well. The music got through. But as we came off stage, Desmond Brown, The Selecter's organ player, started shouting at Andy, 'Don't you ever fucking do that again? You're a cunt if you get scared by an audience.' He obviously had taken umbrage at our nonaggression and was laying it on really thick. 'You can just forget about being in a group or anything, if you let that happen again.' We were all going, 'London is fucking heavy.' How do you weigh that up? We're educating racists? It gave me reason to want to continue. From that night on I had something to fight for and I came to believe that wherever there is racism, Beat music should be played. In its very essence it is anti-racist music.

We never understood why our gigs attracted racists. I remember once a group of about ten skinheads down the front making Nazi-style salutes and throwing coins. I opened my mouth to speak out and one of them spat at me and I got a taste of blackcurrant and lager in my mouth. I was raging mad and jumped off the stage: 'Right… that's it. Come on, which one?' It was tense. The band stopped playing. The road crew ran on stage. Dave was taking off his guitar and David had his bass up above his head ready to whack one of them. I was like, 'Bloody hell. This is heavy.' It was serious and we were ready to fight. The skinheads backed off and we got on with the music and had the troublemakers kicked out. Afterwards, it dawned on me that if one of them had pulled out a knife I could have been seriously injured. It was a wake-up call. The fascists would do it to wind you up. You had to ignore it and show them that you were better than that. From then on I always used the power of the microphone to control a situation. It was a great art to learn. As soon as there was a fight, it was, 'Right, everyone stop. Spotlight on them two now.' Then I'd say, 'What do you lot think of this lot,' and the rest of the audience would boo. 'Okay, you want them out? Let me hear you say "Out... out... out."' You'd get a big cheer and then go into the next number. Oddly, sometimes a little fight was better for the gig. It brought everybody out of their shells and loosened everybody up, but we never encouraged it. One time, a big skinhead came up to me and said, 'I used to be a member of the British Movement, right? But tonight I've seen unity, so fuck 'em!' I told Dave that and we were just smiling because we'd achieved something.

The following month we played with The Selecter again, with a new all-girl group called the Mo-dettes, at the Electric Ballroom in Camden. It was the biggest night of the tour. It was the same day as the newly formed Selecter's 'On My Radio' was released backed with 'Too Much Pressure', and we were told Jerry Dammers was going to be there. It was October 1979, and 2 Tone was on the verge of sweeping the country. News of the gig spread and it was packed with record and publishing companies. We finished our set and Jerry appeared backstage carrying a briefcase. He had a big smile on his face. He said, 'Well done! We want you to do the next 2 Tone single.' We all went, 'Whoa!' Then he said, 'We've got to do it quick. If you can do it in a week we can get it out before Christmas.' We were like, 'WHAT!!'

Around the same time as The Beat started playing with Selecter, we met a man who would go on to play a critical role in the fortunes of the band's commercial success. We first

75

met John Peel at Aston University in June 1979. The gig has become legendary in Beat folklore. The student union asked us to open up for him and we were all excited – 'Let's do it!' We did the gig and the crowd went absolutely mad. They really loved it. They were shouting for more but we only knew ten songs and we had played them all. Peel came onto the stage, and said, 'You don't want to hear me any more. This is the best band in the universe… after The Undertones. Let's have them back again!' I went up to the mic and shouted, 'If you want more, ball out for more… ball out.' Then I said, 'D'you wanna see the Bullfrog? Well, ball out for the Bullfrog.' The Bullfrog was a funny face I used to pull by holding my eyes open with my fingers and puffing my cheeks out; I used to do it at school to make my friends laugh. You can see it in the video of 'Drowning'. I did the Bullfrog and then the rest of the band came out and we did the set again. The crowd went absolutely mad again and were still demanding more. We came back on for a second encore and played 'Mirror In The Bathroom' for the third time. To top it all, at the end, John walked up the mic and said, 'These poor guys are getting paid £50 for doing this and I'm being paid £400. I'm going to swap the cheques.' It was a fantastic thing for him to do. Peel was like royalty to us and we really hit it off. After the gig, we took him to the Butt Sweet Centre in Balsall Heath for a curry. It was such a great night. We had had one of the best gigs a band could have in front of John Peel, our favourite Radio 1 DJ. And then, while we were tucking into our baltis, we discovered our van had got hit by a passing vehicle. The damage ended up costing £400 – the exact amount Peel had exchanged with us.

Peel was responsible for our first major break when he offered us a session on his late-night radio programme. The John Peel Show was the most important show of the week. Anyone who had any music credibility listened to it. Peel may have played weird tracks and unsigned bands but it was always better than daytime pop radio. It was exciting to go to the BBC. When we arrived at the studio in Maida Vale – on October 24, 1979 – the first person to introduce himself was Bob Sargeant, the session producer. It was the most professional studio I'd ever been in. Orchestras used it. I remember thinking, 'This is fantastic.' We went into the BBC canteen and for about two quid you could get a good quality three-course meal. For a band on the dole it was heaven.

Peel wasn't there, so Bob was charged with making our sound good enough for radio broadcast. I was in the control room when Everett and David were warming up and Bob was just tapping his pen on the desk. Eventually, he said to Everett, over the microphone, 'Okay, you need to keep the tempo the same all the way through. It's changing.' Everett was never the steadiest drummer in the world. His tempo would always fluctuate, especially when it came to a drum roll. He'd speed up and the bass would have to catch up with him. Bob did a great job because he got the best out of Everett. We renamed him Uncle Bob. He was a very cool guy. We liked him because he was friendly and he seemed to know what we were about.

It was meant to happen. Our sound wouldn't have been the same without him. He had his own way of doing it but he tried not to suppress the band sound and he kept us organised. We had all these ideas and he would say, 'Keep it as simple but as melodic as possible.' He always tried to get everybody involved and was a master in the art of diplomacy. Bob made our music make sense.

We recorded 'Mirror In The Bathroom', 'Click Click', 'Ranking Full Stop', 'Tears Of A Clown' and 'Big Shot'. The session came out really well. Peel was really happy; I heard the session on the radio at home a week or so later, and he said, 'A few months ago I went to do a gig at Aston University. I mentioned it at the time, it was one of those gigs that turned out to be infinitely better than you could ever have imagined that they would be, mainly because I had nothing to do having written myself out of the script as soon as I saw the band and got them to play through their set twice because they were so good.'

The Peel Session helped to earn us the title of 'the next 2 Tone band'. We said to Bob, 'We've been offered the opportunity to make a single for 2 Tone. Would you produce it?' He jumped at the chance. Bob was dying to leave the BBC and he would go on to produce all of our records over the next four years.

Part Two:
Punky Reggae Party

Rude Boys Don't Argue

2 Tone. Saxa. Tears Of A Clown

There was something bubbling in the Midlands. In Birmingham there were UB40 and Steel Pulse, both with a Jamaican reggae vibe. And in Coventry there were The Specials and The Selecter playing modernised updates of ska with a punk-rock injection. We were doing this sped-up reggae thing which was close to ska, but it wasn't ska. It was more punk and reggae. The Beat was a hybrid mixing reggae, punk and even elements of The Velvet Underground. We were slower and groovier and didn't have guitar solos like the other bands. It was all rhythm and melody. People would say, 'They're not as ska as The Selecter and The Specials, but they are a bit... they're punky-reggae.'

Around 1978 there was a mod revival, largely initiated by the emergence of The Jam and the release of the film *Quadrophenia*. The resurgence of interest in Sixties music and clothes fed into what we were all doing, and that was ultimately validated by Jerry Dammers describing his teenage self as a 'mini-mod' and pinpointing his desire to be in a band at the moment he first saw The Who performing 'My Generation' on *Ready Steady Go!* 2 Tone was going backwards with a forward message. The Selecter did 'Carry Go Bring Come' by Justin Hinds & The Dominoes and The Specials did 'Too Much Too Young', which owed much to 'Birth Control' by Lloydie & The Lowbites. They adapted ska rhythms and played them with a punkier edge, just as all the original Jamaican musicians modified New Orleans jazz music by shifting the accent to the offbeat to create the original ska sound with its cross rhythm. There's a great story about how the founding fathers of ska, The Skatalites, were named. It was at the height of the space race and the name 'Satellites' was suggested as an appropriate comment on the times. But Tommy McCook, the band leader, said, 'No, we play ska. We'll be The *Ska*-talites.'

2 Tone bands bought ska forward to a new audience and wrote about topical social concerns, and together with a punk edge created a new type of music. People were always saying, 'What's the difference between a rude boy and a mod?' In Jamaica, a rude boy was a bad man who dressed slick, like a gangster: white shirt, slim tie, a tonic suit, and maybe a trilby or a pork pie hat. The Specials adopted the fashion and it was simultaneously embraced by both The Selecter and Madness. It gave 2 Tone a look. The rule of The Beat was: dress to suit

yourself. Andy would wear a flowery shirt and the next day he'd be wearing a suit and tie. Dave and I might wear a suit or the next day a T-shirt. We all found our own fashion. I wanted to be different and wear something unique.

After the release of 'Gangsters' it seemed like all my friends became rude boys overnight: they shaved off their mohicans and started to wear three-button tonic suits bought cheaply from second-hand clothes shops or in the Rag Market in town. My friend, Patrick, who was black, became a skinhead and joined the National Front. He cropped his hair, started wearing Levi jeans and Dr. Martens, and pinned an 'NF' badge on his denim jacket. I couldn't believe it. I thought, 'What's happened?' It was strange how fashion could change people. For a few years it was hard to tell who was a rude boy, a skinhead, or a fascist. These were guys who had lived for punk: 'We're going to be punks forever.' It's amazing that one Specials tune had so much effect. Everywhere you went people were suddenly wearing black and white. You couldn't tell apart the police from 2 Tone fans. Whilst rude boys appeared across the country, other punks became skinheads, and that's when, in my opinion, the racism started. Many of the skinheads were attracted to Jimmy Pursey with the misplaced belief that his band, Sham 69, was racist. But I don't believe it was as simple as people often argue, that music turned kids to right-wing politics; the racism I experienced was passed down generationally; from parents to their children.

* * *

We had been doing gigs and going down very well but something was missing. Three days before we recorded our first single we found Saxa, the missing piece in The Beat jigsaw. As a warm up for the recording session, we were booked to play at a party at the Bournebrook in Selly Oak, where we had played our second gig for the handsome sum of £50. On the day of our return to the venue I got in the van and there was this old guy sitting on the back seat wearing a floppy hat and earrings. He was at least thirty years older than any of us. Dave said, 'This is Saxa. He's a friend of Everett's.' The others had been to see him play saxophone with a resident jazz band at the Crompton Arms in Handsworth and persuaded him to come and play with us. At the soundcheck, David Steele said to Saxa, 'Wanna know the keys we're in?' Saxa said, 'Cha! You just play and me'll blow.' I was like, 'Who is this loud mouth… I don't like this guy.' Saxa was friendly enough but he was loud and insistent: 'Get me another drink. What time are we going on?' He was a proper old Jamaican guy. Then he took out his saxophone and started warming up. I instantly felt my irritation melting. It was the way he blew the horn. A saxophone can sound very honky but Saxa's tone was flowing. It sounded like water drops. He had this warm, unique and distinctive sound but all I could hear him saying was, 'Get me another brandy. Get me another brandy.' I was thinking, 'What! In this band everyone's cool.' That was the beauty of The Beat. All these amazing things were happening around us, yet every one of us had our feet on the ground. We went on stage and once Saxa started blowing you couldn't stop him. The crowd went mad. It sounded amazing. He was playing jazz mixed in with calypso mixed over punky reggae and improvising riffs. Everything was spontaneous. We came off stage and Saxa was in raptures: 'You boys are the band for me. I've waited all my life for you boys. Me drop dead on stage with you boys. We's boy's musicians.'

Saxa was born Lionel Augustus Martin in Croft's Hill, Clarendon Parish, Jamaica. He went to the Alpha Boys School with the legendary trombone players Rico Rodriguez and Don Drummond, and lived on Beeston Street, near downtown Kingston. Saxa came to England in the late Fifties and travelled with bands all over the UK. Legend has it that he played with The Beatles at a late-night drinking den in Liverpool. That's what Saxa always used to say. It's believable. There were a lot of shebeens in Liverpool, and after a gig, musicians would often want to party. John Lennon would probably just go to a shebeen to score. He was the biggest pot-smoker there was, and certainly George Harrison used to go to blues dances. He loved that vibe and later owned property in the Caribbean. Typically, a shebeen would have a small drum kit set up and a visiting band would play three or four numbers. Saxa would never remember names of bands or titles of songs. When he heard a melody or a tune, he would say, 'Me did play upon that one.' You'd say, 'Oh, wow!' And it would be a Skatalites tune. Whether or not he played with The Beatles remains a mystery – we can only take him on his word.

By late 1979, 2 Tone was the biggest youth movement since punk. It swept across the nation and began to impact on the charts. I didn't see the first 2 Tone Tour with The Specials, The Selecter and Madness because it clashed with our own gigs. And the celebrated night when all three bands appeared on *Top of the Pops,* we were playing at the Rock Garden in Covent Garden. The poster billed us as 'Birmingham's latest hot export in the Two Tone ska/reggae vein. Recommended!' It was the right time.

Before Jerry offered us a deal at the Electric Ballroom, we had sent a recently recorded demo tape with 'Ranking Full Stop', 'Tears Of A Clown' and a new version of 'Mirror In The Bathroom' to a couple of record labels, but it was obvious that Jerry Dammers was the man for our kind of music. It was like, 'Hang on. 2 Tone is only down the road. We might as well send them something and see what happens.' I later learnt that signing to 2 Tone was a toss-up between us and UB40. During the 2 Tone Tour, Jerry played both bands' demos to everybody on the coach and The Beat won out. Juliet de Valero, the manager of The Selecter, said The Beat were more of a natural fit and that I summed up the youthful energy of 2 Tone, jumping all over the place on stage.

We felt privileged to be asked to record for the label and become the fourth 2 Tone band. Jerry naturally wanted us to record 'Mirror In The Bathroom' as our debut single, but as I mentioned earlier, 2 Tone, despite giving the appearance of an independent label, was licensed to Chrysalis Records, which in turn meant that they would own the rights to our songs for the next five years. We didn't want to give one of our best original songs to a major record label, so we said, 'You can have "Tears Of A Clown" and "Ranking Full Stop".' I also seem to remember David Steele saying 'Mirror In The Bathroom' had 'quite depressing, hard lyrics' and it wouldn't be very popular leading up to Christmas.

At Jerry's suggestion, it was decided that we should record at Horizon Studios in Coventry with Roger Lomas, to follow on from the success he had had with the single mix of The Selecter's 'On My Radio'. All the 2 Tone singles to date had been recorded at Horizon, but as soon as we arrived at the studio we didn't like it. Foremost in our reservations were the continual technical problems. We got to the end of 'Ranking Full Stop' where I say *I said stop* and the track just kept playing over and over. We said, 'We want to use our own producer. We don't want to sound like The Specials and The Selecter anyway. We don't want the 2 Tone sound.' So we left. That was the thing with The Beat. We had to do our thing our way. Bob Sargeant suggested we record at Sound Suite studios in London and we took his advice.

Once relocated to London the band started by playing live to record the rhythm section. We did three takes of 'Tears Of A Clown' and a couple of takes of 'Ranking Full Stop'. Then we did guitar and vocal overdubs. I was ecstatic knowing we were recording a 2 Tone single. It spurred us on and we knew we had to try our hardest and be the best we could ever be. All that was running through our minds. 'This is our chance. We mustn't abuse it. Go with it.' I felt really lucky.

During the recording, Bob couldn't understand a word Saxa said. He hadn't integrated with hardcore-speaking Jamaican people before and I had to interpret until Bob got used to Saxa's slogans and terminology. At the end of the session he just said, 'What a character!' Saxa was a character. A total one-off. I've never met anyone else like him. He could also be a pain in the arse and he always wanted more money and would be late for the bus and turn up everywhere on 'black man time'. Over time, he became the mentor of the band and taught us about morals. He was a big drinker and smoker and often what he said took a while to make sense of. Saxa would talk in parables, and say things like, 'One hand watch the other,' or 'It shall worse and worse,' or when he saw a woman he liked, 'Pretty as money.' He was a very godly man. He was always talking about the Father. He never tried to push it on anyone but you knew where he stood.

With 'Tears Of A Clown' in the bag, 'Ranking Full Stop' was my big moment. The title itself means nothing. It was just a title. I've always seen it more as a dance:

I will really, really tell you and show you how to do the
  Ranking Full Stop
I say you move to your left and then you move to your right.

87

People would see me on the street, and say, 'Look! There's Ranking Full Stop.' I'd have to say, 'No, I'm called Ranking Roger.'

At the end of the session we were each given an acetate: a piece of plastic that you could play on a record player about five times before it would start to deteriorate. You had to tape the acetate onto a cassette on the first play and then you could listen to it over and over. When I saw the first pressing of 'Tears Of A Clown' and 'Ranking Full Stop' with the black-and-white paper label in a 2 Tone sleeve bag, I was like, 'It's coming out! We're part of the movement!'

2 Tone catapulted us into the limelight. It was all happening for us. Everyone was interested. In November, we played a few dates in and around London. The first at the Lyceum supporting Teardrop Explodes and The Human League. Adrian Thrills reviewed our set in the *NME* although he mistakenly credited 'Jackpot' as an original:

'The Beat, the latest link in the 2 Tone chain. Hailing from Birmingham, this multi-racial six-piece have a lot to live up to, but they're doing more than alright because not many bands could follow The Specials, Madness and The Selecter and acquit themselves as well as this bunch. Not as up-front dynamic as any of their stable mates, nor as impressive visually, they compensated for this shortcoming with an engaging and atmospheric hybrid of reggae, soul and R'n'B punk. Their forthcoming single 'Tears Of A Clown' gives a misleading indication of where they are heading. Their own self-penned efforts like 'Jackpot' and 'Ranking Full Stop', the toasted flip of the single, are far superior.'

After the Lyceum gig, I remember standing in the audience with David Steele listening to The Human League. We thought they were cool. David nudged me, and said, 'Here you are,' and passed me a joint. I took a couple of draws and said, 'What is this?' He said, 'It's magic mushrooms.' The Human League never sounded better and I fell in love with Phil Oakey's voice.

As the single was being pressed, more gigs followed in Canning Town, at the Hope & Anchor in Islington, and at Surrey University with John Peel again. It was timed perfectly. The week before, Peel had aired our latest session and read out the tour dates and some details about the band. It was hilarious because Bob Sargeant had written out a brief biography of the band for him but he couldn't read his handwriting. Peel said 'Dave *Wakening* on guitar and lead vocals,' and I was described as, 'Ranking Roger on percussion, vocal and style...' He finished off by saying, 'You ought to see them live, devastating they are.'

'Tears Of A Clown' was released in the first week of December at the most competitive time of the year in the music industry calendar. All the big stars, like Queen and Paul McCartney, were releasing their Christmas hits. The Police were at number one with 'Walking On The Moon', Pink Floyd's 'Another Brick In The Wall' was at number two and Donna Summer and Barbara Streisand were at number three with their duet 'No More Tears (Enough Is Enough)'. 'Tears Of A Clown' entered the chart at number sixty-seven. It was pure joy and a lot of, 'Wow!' and, 'I can't believe it!' We'd never been in the charts before. It was brilliant. 2 Tone and Chrysalis did a great job. It was slow and hard but they knew the song just needed time. The life of a single then was about six weeks and it took four weeks to get up into the Top 10. I remember saying, after it got to number twenty, in its third week, 'It's getting really good.' The music business may have been shutting down for Christmas but our single kept on selling. We'd be in the van going, 'Oh my God! They're playing it again! Amazing!' We never got fed up with hearing it. The more we got played the better because we were in competition with everyone else. And then when they got fed up of playing 'Tears Of A Clown' they would flip the record over and play 'Ranking Full Stop' instead. To hear patois on Radio 1 was unheard of. Tony Blackburn might not have been able to understand what I was saying but he could hear it was a jolly, happy-go-lucky song. To get into the Top 20 was good enough but when it went to number six, 'Wow!' That was really significant and something to behold.

I had only joined the band in March and nine months later we were sailing up the charts and set to make our debut performance on *Top of the Pops*. Between us we had all been signing on and off the dole to different degrees throughout the year, which meant going to the DHSS every week, on the Coventry Road. By the time of The Selecter tour all the band had signed off. It was a risk but I was glad to see the back of it. And then I was due to be on *Top of the Pops*. I thought to myself, 'What a lucky bastard!' I still think that to this day: some great accidents have happened to me. It just felt like I had a knack for being in the right places at the right time.

Every Thursday night, since I could remember, my sisters and I would sit round the television and check out the latest hits and fashions on *Top of the Pops*. Earlier in the year I'd seen The Specials doing 'A Message To You Rudy' with Neville in his Judge Roughneck outfit rolling about the stage and Jerry pretending to play guitar whilst doing Pete Townshend windmill impressions... *Rude Boy don't argue...* I knew the whole nation was going to be watching, including Mum and my sisters and all the kids and teachers at my old school. It was a moment to show everybody what I had achieved. But truth be told I was absolutely crapping myself. The feeling of appearing on national television was total fear.

People used to think bands played live on *Top of the Pops* but it was all miming. As we became more successful we began to learn the shtick: on a Tuesday you would find out your chart position and then on the Wednesday you had to go down to London to pre-record your performance. Due to union regulations the BBC were not allowed to broadcast an original recording. It meant you had to go to a designated studio and re-record your song. When the official from the BBC came to check everything was in order we would swap the tapes over, put a bit of extra reverb on the original record,

91

and say, 'This is the finished track.' All the bands did it. Or sometimes you would just re-record the lead vocal over the original backing track. When a song sounded different on air was when a group hadn't got away with switching the master tapes. But as far as *Top of the Pops* was concerned, in the studio and to the viewer: bands were playing live.

When we arrived at the BBC for our inaugural appearance we did two rehearsals with cameras and the third time was with the studio audience. The cameramen was saying, 'When you see the red light on the top of a camera, look at that one.' I was learning in the moment: 'Oh, okay!' I remember overhearing the warm-up presenter saying to the audience, 'Twenty million people will be watching when it's broadcast on Thursday night...' That was almost half the population of the UK in 1979. You figure that into your thinking and it's not psychologically good for a debut performance. I was like, 'Woah! Thank God we are miming.' Mike Read introduced us, saying, 'In 1970 Smokey Robinson & The Miracles had 'Tears Of A Clown' at number one. There's a new version out which is heading in that direction by a great new group. It's The Beat.' The song started and I didn't know what to do. If you watch the footage you can see I was hit by nerves. About thirty seconds into the song I remembered I had been told, 'Make sure you smile.' All of a sudden I was grinning like a Cheshire Cat.

To our delight, we received a telegram from Smokey Robinson. He wrote that he had heard 'six different versions of

"Tears Of A Clown" already this year. May I congratulate you on recording the best version.' Despite 'Tears Of A Clown' being such a big song in my life I'm sad to say I've never met Smokey Robinson. Years later, Dave met him and said that Smokey gave him a big hug that went on for ages, but I don't think any of the other members have had the privilege. If I'm honest, I actually prefer Smokey's recording of 'Tracks Of My Tears'.

On December 20, The Specials hastily organised a show at Tiffany's in Coventry to be filmed for a forthcoming BBC *Arena* documentary on 2 Tone. We were invited to support, and by coincidence it was the same night our recording of 'Tears Of A Clown' on *Top of the Pops* was broadcast. It made for a magical night. When we arrived, Saxa decided to walk through the crowd and everybody wanted to talk to him. The crowd was buzzing and you could see pork pie hats and cheap second-hand tonic suits everywhere. It was one of the best gigs we ever played. The crowd went mad and we were on fire. You can find the documentary, *Rudies Come Back*, online, featuring fantastic footage of The Specials performing 'A Message To You Rudy', 'Stupid Marriage' – with Neville Staple dressed as Judge Roughneck – and 'You're Wondering Now', and complete with an interview in 2 Tone headquarters including an hilarious moment when Jerry Dammers accidentally pulls down a clothes rail of the band's stage suits.

After Christmas we were invited back on to *Top of the Pops*. Second time round, a cameramen said to me, 'When you sing *tears of a clown I'm going down de Crown*, blow this party popper.' It was stupid but because it was New Year I reasoned it made sense, and it helped to lighten my heavy Jamaican accent on the play-out of the record. A significant memory I have of *Top of the Pops* is the change of my appearance. Up to that point I was still going on stage wearing a leather jacket and bondage trousers. It was time to find a new image. I decided to step into the 2 Tone look and like many of my friends before me went from being a punk to a rude boy overnight. I bought a shirt and a trilby from Dunn & Co. on Bull Street – hats suited me and I collected half-a-dozen before Dunn's closed down a couple of years later – and a second-hand green-and-purple-tinted tonic suit. As The Beat became more successful, clothes were often sent to us and Tyler's had three or four suits made to measure for me. I wore one of their suits when we did a Trades Union Congress 'Rock for Jobs' double-headline gig with UB40 at Bingley Hall in 1981. The night was heaving: we went on first and mashed it up – but I'm getting ahead of myself.

'Tears Of A Clown' was 2 Tone's fourth consecutive hit. We had signed a one-single deal with an option to do an album but when it came to the crunch we didn't want to be a 2 Tone band. With the benefit of hindsight, we would have gone down with the rest of it. Maybe it would have been good to stay with 2 Tone and rule the roost with The Specials. But we had to do our own thing, branch out and expand, and ride on our own wheels. In all truth, we were never in the 2 Tone line of music, but 'Tears Of A Clown' was great for them. It was punky reggae and broke up the ska sound of The Specials, The Selecter and Madness. We advanced the perception of 2 Tone and made them look more like a broad-minded label. I'd gone through punk and new wave hot on its heels: Elvis Costello & The Attractions, The Police, Blondie. Everybody wanted to do ska. By the time of 2 Tone, I thought, 'It's a fashion and fashions only last for so long.' That's why after buying into the 2 Tone suit-and-tie look I then got a bigger hat and began to move away from the rude boy image. We became our own thing.

With a massive hit to our name, the music industry smelt money and all of a sudden we had eight, nine, ten record companies circling around us: 'We want to sign you up,' 'We'll give you £½ a million,' 'We'll give you £1 million.' EMI came with an open cheque and simply said, 'You guys write the figure.' A 2 Tone hit single was that big. We were the latest thing but we didn't trust any of them. Then, Tarquin Gotch introduced himself. He was head of A&R for Arista Records. He came to the Electric Ballroom and a Birmingham club date at the Underworld Club wearing a Crombie and pork pie hat. It impressed us. Tarquin was playing our game. He was the most sincere out of all the record company people we met and really wanted to sign the band. He said, 'We know you've been offered £1 million. We can't offer that much. But we can give you as much freedom as you want. We'll even offer you your own record label.' For us, it wasn't about the money. We had a punk mentality. It was about freedom. That was crucial. We were never the kind of band that if you put limousines in front of us or nice boats we'd jump for them. Times were hard and you needed money to survive, but in our eyes money didn't equal happiness; money equalled freedom. It allowed you to do what you wanted. I remember Dave saying how punk bands had been exploited by the major labels. What was different about Arista was that they came to the table and reasoned with us. They didn't tell us what to do and they tried to make things work halfway. Looking at our peers, The Selecter had stayed with The Specials on 2 Tone, and after the 'The Prince', Madness had signed to Stiff Records. We wanted our own record label. And so Go Feet Records was born.

Jerry said that 2 Tone was an opportunity to 'give our mates a chance too'. That's how we felt about Go Feet. It was a playground for us. 'Let's have a label like 2 Tone with our own identity and release music that we like.' And it gave us control over our own music and production and artwork. The name Go Feet was based on dance and the label was licensed through Arista. After the Christmas holidays we did the deal. Once we had signed the contract, instead of being taken out to a posh French restaurant near Arista's offices in Mayfair, what did The Beat ask for? McDonald's! It was the punk spirit of doing the opposite. Forty years ago, McDonald's was pretty new to England, so we were like, 'Wow! Let's go there. Big

Mac and a Shake!' It was mad but we were young and naïve.
We signed to Arista for about £150,000 and we were all put
on a monthly wage of about £750. It was high for what it
should have been. We were like middle-class pop stars. I
would give £3,000 or maybe £5,000 to Mum and then bank
the rest towards buying a house. I had a little nest egg but I
was also a big spender.

With a new record deal it also felt like the right time to
get a new manager. Mick Hancock had been looking after
the band for the past year. I liked him but we were not happy
with the way he was running things. He had a big chance,
but I think he may have had problems outside of the band.
Things get in the way and stop you, but if you're passionate
about something you don't let anything stop you. You get
on with it and you get through. We were all passionate. We
were taking a big risk. One day we wanted him for something
and we couldn't find him, so we told him he was rubbish and
he wasn't paying enough attention to what he was doing.
Instead we asked our agent, John Mostyn, to manage us.
John had booked gigs for The Specials from their early days
and was looking to do something different and move into
management. We went with him because we wanted to work
with people we thought we could trust. We knew there were
a lot of sharks around and John seemed very honest. He
would tell you it as it was. If it wasn't happening he would
say so. John set up 20/21 Music – a reference to the postcode
districts of Handsworth – to manage The Beat and he got

97

all the deals for us. John brought in Jayne Davies, who had purple dyed hair and was a great organiser. They set up office in a third floor flat, a stone's throw from the Soho Road, above where we would later build our own rehearsal room. 1980 was destined to be our year.

Mr Full Stop

Ranking Full Stop. Sexism. Hands Off...
She's Mine

In January, we played our first hometown gig since hitting the charts with 'Tears Of A Clown'. The Beat always refused to play seated venues and the Top Rank was the only all-standing venue in Birmingham with a capacity of over 2,000. We had been to see so many bands there and it was a full house. As we walked out of the dressing room towards the stage I could sense how scared we all were. We had about an hour's worth of songs and did the whole set in about twenty minutes. 'Hands Off...She's Mine' must have sounded like 'Click Click'; ninety seconds of punk thrash. My sisters were in the audience and they brought along Dad. After the gig he told me he didn't like it very much, but over the years he's relaxed his opinion and now loves us. Beat music is like Clash music. It takes a few listens. Mum didn't see the band until later in the year. She was just pleased music had kept me out of prison. I had always wanted to be famous but I didn't think the band would get as big as quickly as it did. I was about to turn seventeen and we were being talked about as pop stars. How do you get that into your head and remain normal? I allowed it for a brief hour. And then instead of exploding and doing somersaults I kept it down. We were all excited about our impact into the pop world but it was important to stay grounded and control it, otherwise we would have lost sight of what we were doing. I was just so thankful for being there. I've always felt that the day I get boastful or become big-headed I'll lose my talent.

Following Birmingham, we played dates in Bournemouth and Brighton and then returned to the Electric Ballroom, where Jerry had offered us the 2 Tone single deal. It coincided with 2 Tone's first number one record. I first heard 'Too Much Too Young' on *Top of the Pops* when they showed a video of The Specials playing it live. The next thing it shot to number one, knocking The Pretenders' 'Brass In Pocket' off the top spot. It captured the whole excitement of the movement. With all these tunes crashing into the charts it was opening up the eyes of the populace to reggae-influenced music. Yet, despite the commercial success of the 2 Tone bands, racism at gigs was on the increase. Of all the bands, The Specials, and particularly, Neville Staple and Lynval Golding, got the most abuse from audiences. As much as I celebrated The Specials' success we chose to distance ourselves from the label and pulled out of the second 2 Tone Tour with The Selecter and The Bodysnatchers. It was brilliant to have an all-girl ska band – just the fact that the girls were having a crack at it; in time they would have learnt their instruments – but it wasn't helping us to be continually associated with the negative media image of 2 Tone, which suggested gigs were overrun by skinheads and Nazis. Yes, there was a small minority of idiots who attempted to disrupt gigs but it was a symptom of the time. Punk bands and mod revivalists had their share of troublemakers to deal with too, but perhaps 2 Tone attracted notoriety in the media because of its commercial success.

At the Lyceum, UB40 supported us and a new group from Hull called Akrylykz, who had just released their first single, 'Spyderman'. We all really liked Akrylykz. Roland Gift was their saxophone player. I remember him as the quiet one but we got on with one another and they became one of our favourite support bands. When I heard Roland sing in the Fine Young Cannibals a few years later, I was like, 'What! I didn't know he could do that.'

Sounds reviewed the London date, but Pete Silverton was unimpressed:

'Ranking Roger's nonsensical, hand-me-down vocal blatherings and counting up how many times he shouted "Hip, hip, hip" was my only diversion. If Benny Hill ever decides to do a skit on a Rasta toaster, he needn't dress himself up at all. He could just use it Rankin' Roger straight. Oh, OK, I'm being unfair. He had a great hat – black with wide flat brims. Gregory Isaacs has got one just like it, only he cheats by being able to sing as well.'

The following night we played the Lyceum with The Selecter and Secret Affair. It was a children's charity gig organised by Capital Radio. We played 'Pussy Price Gone Up' and Laurel Aitken, who originally cut the record in 1969, joined us on stage and the crowd went wild. For this gig, Paul Du Noyer reviewed us in *NME* and made a comment about the similarity between 'Pussy Price Gone Up' and 'Ranking Full Stop'. It may be that part of the bass line bears a similarity but it was a totally different tune. Aitken tried to take The Beat to court on the grounds that 'Ranking Full Stop' was his tune. I said, 'You tell me where your lyrics are on there?'

The Original Africans had a tune called 'Mr Full Stop' written by Eddy Grant, which we used to play in the early days and was possibly where the idea for 'Ranking Full Stop' originated. We were trying to learn new tunes all the time or jamming stuff like 'Conscious Man' or Millie Small's 'My Boy Lollipop'. Dave said, 'All right then, Roge. Here you go, these are the lyrics.' I was like, 'What do you mean, these are the lyrics? You want me to toast another man's words. I can't do that. I've got my own style.'

The first time we tried to record 'Ranking Full Stop' was for the Peel Session before we were signed. The only lyrics I had were:

102

Are you ready
Are you ready to go
Are you ready
Are you ready to stop

I went into the studio and recorded two totally different takes, freestyle, mixing 'Mr Full Stop' in with 'Ranking Full Stop', and I just kept toasting with the music going round and round until I gave the cue to finish the song by saying *are you ready to stop*. All these years later, I often do 'Pussy Price Gone Up' with the current line-up of The Beat as a medley with 'Ranking Full Stop' because both songs have the same chords. I sing:

One time you get it for twenty cent
Now if you follow pussy, you can't pay your rent
Why? Pussy price gone up

And then:

Full Stop. Ranking Full Stop

And the crowds go mad.

It was old Jamaican songs like 'Pussy Price' that led some feminists to accuse us of being sexist. When we did 'Rough Rider' I would toast:

She was a rough rider, a rough rider
Tell ya about the sound, you better drink up your cider
Me take off my jeans and she starting to scream
Take off my brief and then she says 'Good grief! What a brand
new release' A wor!

Rather than sexist we thought they were sexy. And many women agreed with us. But local accusations came to a head when we were due to play with the Au Pairs. We designed a poster with a muscular-looking torso of a woman holding a whip, with a tattoo on her arm branded with 'Au Pairs' and 'The Beat'. We pasted the posters around Moseley Village and Lesley [Woods] and her manager ripped them all down, knocked on our door, and threw them all at Dave, shouting, 'Sexists.' We told the others what had happened in rehearsal and decided as a joke it would be funny to play a cover version of Prince Buster's 'Whine And Grine' at the gig, which referenced *a ruff rider* and *a cool stroker*, to wind Lesley up.

The Au Pairs got the joke and continued to open up for us quite a lot over the next few years. The great thing about Lesley was, when she had a point to make, she spoke her mind and never held back. That's what I loved about her. I heard her interviewed on the radio more recently and she was brilliant. I feel privileged to have known her back then. Lesley never called me sexist even though I was the one toasting many of the words that she objected to. Generally, I was seen as the happy-go-lucky black punk who picked up the mic and got on with everyone, and it was becoming a member of The Beat that also began to change my view of different people's oppression. I would laugh at something and then notice nobody else joining in. It would make me think, 'Oh, maybe I'm doing the wrong thing then.' I was learning new ways of being.

With MCing, I was never sexist in a derogative or an explicit way. Some songs were on the edge but generally I was well behaved. The boys would make sure: 'You can't say that, Roge. Try something a bit more subtle.' I was young and needed pulling back. They made me aware and careful about what I wrote. With the growth of Rock Against Racism there was a growing sense of challenging all oppression against minorities. Sexism was at the top of the agenda. We were lined up to do an interview for Rock Against Racism's fanzine *Temporary Hoarding* just after we recorded a slot on *LOOK! HEAR!*, a local TV programme at Pebble Mill Studios presented by Toyah Wilcox. During the filming there was a stand-off between exuberant dancers and the BBC, resulting in the police being called and fans being escorted off the premises. I was really annoyed with both the treatment of the band and the audience, so I went home. It left Dave and David to defend The Beat over our imminent new single 'Hands Off...She's Mine' in *Temporary Hoarding [TH]*:

DAVID: They're probably the worst lyrics in the set.

DAVE: Probably. It was a real-life situation. Totally corny, totally ridiculous, but when you get involved with girls you tend to do such stupid things...

TH: You think you can possess someone, say *she's mine*.

DAVE: Oh, I see why you object now.

DAVID: But it's a love song really.

TH: Depends on your definition of 'love'.

DAVE: Have you ever gone out with someone and walked in to find him with another girl? Don't you feel hurt?

TH: I don't feel I can *own* anyone.

DAVID: That's myopic, if you don't mind me saying. If you want to hold someone, that's not domination.

DAVE: I mean, if you take everything literally some women would object to us using the word 'cunt' in the anti-Nazi song.

TH: Yes.

DAVE: But it's just a swear word used for effect. I think we get across to a lot more girls, than, say, the Au Pairs, anyway.

TH: What do you get across?

DAVID: Well, we don't sing about raping women or strut around. I hate macho men anyway. They're vile. Men and women are oppressed by the roles forced upon them. I don't think we're a sexist band.

TH: And this song?

DAVE: It's meant to be a spoof.

The conversation carried on in the same vein for hours and Rock Against Racism wrapped up by saying that when they took David home he looked genuinely scared when a pair of scissors were produced. *Temporary Hoarding* concluded the article by saying: '… [The Beat] must think out their ideas on things like sexism, and make clear unambiguous statements of their views. 2 Tone it's time to take a stand!'

* * *

I call Dave and I the Everly Brothers of ska. We would practise and work out harmonies while the others recorded their instruments. I always say Dave's voice comes from a mix of Elvis Costello and trying to sound like a black singer. Dave was the main lyric writer in The Beat but once I joined the band he was picking up all my buzzwords and sticking them in tunes. I'd pick up something from a record or off the street and when Dave and I sat down and put words together I'd say, 'You know what you should do there, don't you? *I told my friend I fancied you* – don't say that, man, sing *I told me friend I'll check for you*'. Dave was like, 'Fucking hell, that's great, Roge. It sounds like a black man singing.'

Dave and David were both fans of the magazine *Photo-Love Weekly*, which is where the title of 'Hands Off…She's Mine' came from. My contribution to the writing was to add the MCing, which when we recorded was usually captured in one or two takes:

Take your hands off me darta
Come mek I tell you tek you hands off me darta
Come mek I tell you say no mess around on ya
Mek tell you say I don't want ta ketch ya
Brrrraaaah!

In reggae *darta* was 'your girlfriend' but people misunderstood it as *daughter*. I was toasting as the girl's father to complement Dave's lyrics.

A lot of my toasting in The Beat was freestyle. Whatever came into my head I just went with it. I had so many lyrics running around in my brain. I could MC for twenty minutes non-stop. Now, I would repeat myself or run out of ideas. It was what I call 'head top'. I just needed a hook line and a verse. Sometimes you improvise off the bass line but usually you're going against what everything else is doing. Ahead of recording, I would write some ideas down or practise so when they said, in the studio, 'Right Roge, here's your toast bit. Are you ready?' they could press record and I would do a take. 'Hands Off…She's Mine' was done in that way. Automatically. When we did an extended version of 'Hands Off…She's Mine', it offered another lyrical approach.

You're a wonderful person
I tell ya, I admire your mind

How can you admire someone's mind? You admire *someone*, not their mind. There was a lot of quirkiness to think about.

I said, nine months gone and a no baby can't born
And no nappies on the line – a waor!

The intention was to be humorous, and then:

Say I wanna wash the dishes
Come mek a tell ya, say I wanna mop the floor
Come mek a say me, Close the kitchen door and make you
*   ball out fe more*
and then me give ya some urgh – a waor!

It was a piss-take. It was all in good humour. The single version was harder and the extended version was mellower and showed the more female side of the male. Bob Sargeant added a marimba to give the feel of a steel band.

'Hands Off…She's Mine' was slammed by Deanne Pearson in the *NME*: 'it lacks any kick and punch in its arrangement, and any sense in its lyrics, which are sexist drivel about youth club jealousies that betray the band's own narrow-mindedness and suggest a lack of songwriting talent.' Despite the criticism, 'Hands Off…She's Mine' entered the charts at number forty-eight and by March it was in the Top 10. It stayed on the chart for nine weeks. Peter Powell introduced us on *Top of the Pops* with a welcome, positive tone: 'I would defy anybody to sit back when that band's playing… go and see them live if you possibly can.' If somebody was looking closely they would have noticed it was the first time Saxa's son, Lionel, played with us on television. Lionel had been brought in as Saxa's apprentice. He sounded just like his old man. He had meticulously learnt to play all the solos and had a similar tone to Saxa. You knew who had taught him. Lionel would have melded into The Beat beautifully but after a year or so with us on the road he decided being in a band was not what he wanted. Saxa returned for our second *Top of the Pops* as 'Hands Off…She's Mine' climbed, together with several cardboard cut-outs of the newly designed Beat Girl strategically placed across the stage.

We had noticed at 2 Tone gigs, especially with The Specials, that the audience would be 80, 90 per cent male. It was the same with The Selecter, who were seen as a man's band, possibly enforced by Pauline's tomboy image. We wanted to redress the balance and found an old black-and-white picture in *Melody Maker* of Prince Buster dancing with a cool-looking girl. We gave it to illustrator Hunt Emerson and charged him with making a logo for the band with a Sixties feel. Or perhaps it was Hunt who discovered the image. Either way, what he came back with was brilliant. The Beat Girl defined the band and symbolised the balance within The Beat, showing that we had a feminine side, and represented our anti-sexist and anti-racist beliefs.

Hunt was a local comics artist who had seen The Beat before me and Saxa had joined and had suggested he might do a logo or poster design for the band. Before he knew what had hit him he was seconded to provide all the graphics for our record label, tours, adverts, badges, T-shirts. His reward was suddenly seeing girls all over the country dressed as the Beat Girl, entire audiences dressed in red and black, Sting wearing Hunt's design on a T-shirt on *Top of the Pops*, and even a skinhead at a gig with the Beat Girl tattooed on his arm.

Shortly after the Beat Girl began to appear on all our imagery we began to notice more and more women at our shows, and with it the malevolence at our gigs began to subside. I think it was partly to do with moving on from 2 Tone, coupled with the added imagery. In fact, we were frequently told that Beat gigs became a great place to find a girlfriend or boyfriend. The Beat Girl made sense.

Part Three:
This is Beat

Which Side Of The Bed?

I Just Can't Stop It. **Stand Down Margaret**

By late spring, 1980, we had released two singles, both of which had been hits. The next step was to record an album. We went to Ridge Farm, a residential studio in the Surrey countryside, and began to record. Two weeks later, and with a clutch of backing tracks committed to tape, we left and moved to the Roundhouse Studios at 100 Chalk Farm Road, Camden, as they had a new digital 3M 32-track digital recorder.

Prior to the age of digital recording, music was recorded onto two-inch tape. Today, in a world where sound is captured in .wav files and converted to ones and zeroes, the analogue era may appear crazy. Understandably, we were excited to be at the forefront of new technological changes. Bronze Records wanted a young band to test the new equipment at the Roundhouse and we were invited to be the guinea pigs. We relocated to London only to be confronted by machines that kept breaking down. We would be two hours into a session and something would go wrong. It would take an hour for an engineer to arrive and then it would take another two hours to repair the problem. Finally they would get going and then the next day the same thing would happen. There were a lot of teething problems. It was annoying but we were getting a special cut-price rate. In all it took six weeks at a cost of £30,000 to record the album. That was cheap.

The benefit of working in a digital studio was the clinical and pure recorded sound. You could hear every breath, every percussive sound, and every beat. When we were mixing the songs, I remember the engineers moaning that the tape ambience of old was missing: 'The digital has stripped all the outer frequencies.' You didn't hear the dirt and hiss of analogue tape. All that was gone. We had to equalise them back in. Analogue gives a full-bodied sound. However, I would argue that recording digitally only took something away in the same way that if you listened to a vinyl record after only listening to MP3s for twenty years the difference would be enormous.

During the recording sessions we were staying in a small apartment near Marble Arch. The rooms were built for businessmen and were owned by an Arab. We'd get to the Roundhouse around two o'clock in the afternoon with the intention of stopping at midnight, but more often than not, we'd still be there at two or three in the morning. One day I popped my head round the door of the other studio room and saw a girl who I thought looked familiar. She was very slim and had long brown wavy hair. I said, 'Hello,' and she said, 'Hello.' When I came out the others said, 'That was Kate Bush!' I was like, 'WHAT! I knew I recognised her face.' I don't know what Kate was recording but shortly after she released *Never For Ever*, which became not only her first number one album but the first by a British female artist to top the UK charts. When we got bored we'd go up the road to Dingwalls in Camden Market and see bands play. I saw The Cure, and The Ruts, who I performed with a couple of times. As a band, we would dance after the live music had finished; people would come up and say hello but generally they left us alone.

When we wrote the first album nobody could read music. We were all still learning our instruments. It was only when we went out on tour and realised that half of the guitars were clashing that we were like, 'Oh my God, we better get this right.' It would take us until our third album before we could all actually play our instruments properly and knew our tools. It was experience. After doing so many gigs, your voice naturally improves. We were learning about control and introducing new dynamics to our voices, like falsetto. Up to that point everything was done hard and your vocal chords would suffer. You have to find the character of a song. I had to complement Dave's voice and not dominate. We would have many a laugh trying different approaches to harmony singing. It was not really until I did my first solo album, *Radical Departure*, in 1988 that I truly felt confident and could take advantage of the freedom to make all my own decisions. It was a case of practice makes perfect. The first Beat record, we went in blind. No one really knew what they were doing. If you were to take The Beat and strip it down to explain it, you would say, 'It was one big happy jam', and everybody was just guessing what the best thing to play was. When they were working out the songs, or sometimes not until the mixing stage, Andy would say to Dave, 'It's not an A major, it's an A minor seventh. I was like, 'What's one of them, man?'

When you make an album, you go into the studio with an idea of how a song is going to sound and you always came out with something slightly different. Songs grow up in the process of recording and sometimes become something more commercial. The rhythm track would be recorded first and Dave and I would sing along as a guide for the others. My role was to toast and to be an influencer on lyrics and sound structure. I knew what I could hear in my head and would push for it. Dave and Andy were the masters who arranged everything, but I'd put The Beat sound down to Bob Sargeant. We'd come with a jam and a rough arrangement and Bob would iron us out, keep the tempos the same and organise us.

In the live room, the drums were cornered off with sound baffles and David would play bass alongside Everett while I would lie down by the bass bin and take in the rhythms. David came up with all those fantastic hypnotic bass lines on tracks like 'Mirror In The Bathroom' and 'Twist And Crawl'. Bass in reggae is the lead instrument and I used to study his weird lines. I would think, 'What! You can't go there?' But it worked. He really loved reggae and soul, and especially Tamla Motown. He'd studied 'roots, rock, reggae' and made it something else. In rehearsals, I was the only one who was allowed to play David's bass. He loved me because I was always asking for more bottom end in the mix. Later when we cut 'Which Side Of The Bed?' the bass was so heavy it made the needle on people's record players jump.

If 'Tears Of A Clown' and 'Hands Off...She's Mine' had been the commercial sound of The Beat, the album was the political side. I loved The Beat because it was about two sides of the coin, in every way: in subject; in music. It crossed borders and appealed to a socialist conscience or simply to people in relationships, who could say, 'I've experienced that.' We were talking about real things – whether they be political, social or romantic – and our experiences. Punk and reggae lyrics were about social reality. We just updated it to sing about our lives. Songs like 'Two Swords', about racism, or 'Big Shot', which Dave wrote about capitalism after standing in the freezing cold at a bus stop in Five Ways trying to get to work. He said he would watch Rolls-Royces and BMWs go past and the drivers would deliberately steer into puddles and splash everyone in the queue.

Five Ways was the business centre of Birmingham. It was an enormous roundabout with an underpass surrounded by high-rise buildings. At one point, The Beat looked into buying one of the buildings to avoid paying tax. It was against the grain of our beliefs and in the end we pulled out. We also considered investing £5,000 to open Birmingham's first McDonald's franchise in 1983, but again, we didn't like the way the corporation operated. We would have made so much money.

'Can't Get Used To Losing You', written by Doc Pomus and Mort Shuman, was a song we learnt in the studio. I knew the original version by Andy Williams, who had a number two hit with the song in 1963. It was a gem and was another example of the commercial side of The Beat. While we were at the Roundhouse we also considered recording 'Conscious Man', which had been in the live set since the Mercat Cross days, but regrettably we never got round to it. We wanted to capture the Lee Perry sound from the original Jolly Brothers record. Dave and I even tried it in rehearsals for General Public a few years later, but a satisfactory version of the song continued to elude us.

We were all there for the mixing of the first record. Bob listened to each song on a little pair of radio speakers, because that was how the majority of the nation listened to music. The idea came from Berry Gordy, who used to listen to new Motown songs by The Supremes or The Miracles on a transistor radio in his car. People used to say, 'If you want a radio hit it's got to sound good on little speakers.' Actually, Bob had three different sets of speakers in the mixing room and we would switch between them to get the balance right. Alongside the small speakers we had Yamaha NS10s; studio engineers said they were the best mixing speakers in the world because you had to work to get a good sound from them but if you were successful, thereafter a record would sound great on anything. The third set of speakers I called 'the upstairs'. They were huge and gave the best impression of the sound in a nightclub. It was always my intention that The Beat should never sound tinny. When 'Gangsters', by The Specials, came out it was the heavy bass line that first got me. Horace Panter said they had to recut the record because the bass made home stereo needles jump on their record players, so Jerry added a piano part to balance out the sound with a higher frequency. Sadly, when their debut album was released, it lacked bottom end. Elvis Costello did wonders in the production and gave The Specials that edge that made them sound really brash and streetwise and different from anything else out there; but it was also a bit tinny.

An important part of Beat music was the twelve-inch versions we made of our songs. The Eighties was a boom time for the extended mix single; taking the original recorded version and radically changing its presentation to offer fans a fresh variation. After we finished a mix of a song for the album we would work on the dub version. It would usually be me, Andy and Bob Sargeant at the controls. I remember Bob saying, 'What's a dub, Roger?' And the engineer being really worried that I was going to blow his speakers from the sub-bass and overall volume I loved boosting. To get Andy and Bob in the mood I would play them some Lee Perry and Scientists and Prince Jammy. Once they were in the groove they would help me to get down my ideas and generously allowed me to direct the mix. We would do three or four takes, adding echo and reverb and chopping instruments in and out, and then edit between the best versions. The mixing desk had a function called 'total recall' which saved all the original settings from the single version, which meant that if you made a mistake you could go back to the beginning. I was proud of the Beat dub versions. 'Twist And Crawl' was one of The Beat's best dubs. The song was written by David when he lived in the Isle of Wight with a friend of his called Dick Bradsell who wrote the lyrics. We re-laid the original backing track from the single version and then stripped all the instruments out of the mix except the rhythm; by then cutting the bass and drums in and out we could change the feel of the whole track. In 1997, I toasted on a version of 'Twist And Crawl' for Death In Vegas.

'Mirror In The Bathroom' was the first digital single to chart in the UK. We released it at the beginning of May, a fortnight ahead of the album. If I had to reduce The Beat down to one song I would choose 'Mirror In The Bathroom'. In its essence it represents everything I believe about the band. It's a stone cold underground classic but rightfully also stormed up the charts, nestling at number four for two weeks behind Paul McCartney, Dexys Midnight Runners' first number one, 'Geno', and the Eurovision Song Contest winning entry 'What's Another Year' by Johnny Logan. 'Mirror In The Bathroom' sounded so clean and crisp compared to other records being played on the radio. Dave wrote the song about narcissism but when we went to America people thought the references to *glass tables* was about cocaine. For the video we were filmed playing in the famous Rum Runner club on Broad Street in Birmingham, with additional footage made up of us looking into mirrors in a doss house behind the club and in shop windows captured outside C&A on Corporation Street. The video was directed by Juliet McKoen, who was a friend of Dave and Andy's from Bournville Sixth Form College. Juliet made public information films before later directing the award-winning thriller film *Frozen*, in 2005.

As well as 'Mirror In The Bathroom', another much-loved song of ours is 'Stand Down Margaret', for many people the tune that defines The Beat. It's such a chant and to sing it on stage with a packed theatre singing along with you is an awesome experience, particularly during Margaret Thatcher's first term in office as Prime Minister. I was too young to vote in 1979, and although it would have been unusual for a black man to vote Conservative, I knew that many were. I was singing what I believed:

> *I sometimes wonder if I'll ever get the chance*
> *Just to sit wid my children in a holiday jam*
> *Our lives seem pretty in your cold grey hands*
> *Would you give a second thought would you ever give a damn*
> *I doubt it*
> *Stand down Margaret.*

Margaret Thatcher was the only woman who I ever feared. I knew her as 'Thatcher the Milk Snatcher' from her time as Secretary of State for Education and Science, when she cut free school milk to children over the age of seven. Milk was a nutrient and beneficial to poor families. I used to have two or three bottles of milk a day when I was at primary school. When she became the leader of the Conservative Party in 1975, people would say, 'Watch her. She's dangerous. She'll change things.' We didn't like what she stood for. I thought, 'If this woman ever gets into power, God help us.' A year before she was elected Prime Minster she appeared on *World in Action* and said, 'People are really rather afraid that this country might be rather swamped by people with a different culture'. We were used to that kind of racism from the National Front. It was expected, but despite the flagrant racism I thought Thatcher put it mildly. As far back as I could remember, Conservatives had talked of 'too many immigrants in the country' whilst Labour would say the opposite.

Thatcher was clever. And as the first woman Prime Minister she never faltered. My god she was powerful. She was as strong as a steely horse and ruled like a rod of iron. She slammed it down with an iron rod and people felt it. The Conservative government stripped people of everything. They took away all the services, privatised everything and allowed interest rates to soar. By the time we knew where we were it was too late. It was like, 'What have you done? You've sold the country off. Everybody is broke. What are we going to do?'

Everything belonged to the people before. She made changes that the country has never recovered from.

The genesis of 'Stand Down Margaret' grew out of the cover version of 'Whine And Grine' we did when we wanted to wind up Lesley from the Au Pairs. We kept the same rhythm and wrote 'Stand Down Margaret' over it. I was thrilled my toasting was featured on such an important record. It was the political and underground side of The Beat. With music and politics you can only partially put the message over. Even if you know you're right you can't push it down people's throats. The idea of Beat lyrics was to let people decide for themselves. We gave them a story and let the audience make up their own minds. We said, 'What do you think about this?' That was our whole philosophy. We were trying to ask questions and be truthful about what we saw around us. It's about making people aware. It was obvious from the song what we stood for, but we were also saying, 'Decide for yourself.' *Stand down Margaret, please.* It was cleverly done by Dave.

We recorded a dub version and released it as a double A-sided single with 'Best Friend', which Dave and Andy had written in the Isle of Wright. The record sleeve had a mushroom cloud on the back cover behind a robotomorphic image of Margaret Thatcher, designed by Hunt Emerson and Suzy Varty. The sleeve also had the logo and address of the Campaign for Nuclear Disarmament and the Anti-Nuclear Campaign. We thought we should put our money where our mouths were and donate the royalties of the record to both groups. The first cheque was for £15,000 and CND opened an office with the proceeds. Ironically, a further £4,000 was paid in taxes. We also had a poster made that said, 'Nuclear power – no thanks'. I used to go to CND marches and I remained active throughout The Beat; 'Stand Down Margaret' was an opportunity to express what we believed in. We were taking risks and there were times when we thought we were being watched by the government. They probably thought we were communists or subversives. We would see suspicious-looking people at our gigs. It was very scary. You didn't know who was watching you. I largely ignored it because I knew I was singing the truth. Look how much damage nuclear power has done to our world. In 1979 there had been the accident at the Three Mile Island Nuclear Generating Station in Pennsylvania and nuclear war was an ever-present fear. I was only seventeen. I had a genuine sense that Margaret Thatcher could press the nuclear button. We said, 'If you want to kill yourself in war or get blown up and end up looking like a two-headed fish, you carry on.' We were quite happy to be taking risks because by then we had had three Top 10 hits. People expected us to come out and say something. But when you look back at the history of The Beat, 'Stand Down Margaret' was our downfall. It was our first single not to make the Top 20 and the BBC quietly and unofficially banned the song, which we found out from the record company. Yet, forty years, later people remember us for it: 'You stood up to Thatcher.' The women at Greenham Common sang it and we heard the miners singing it on the BBC news during the 1984–5 industrial dispute. I shall always be proud of our song and the stance we took.

The Noise In The World

British and European tour. The Police

In May 1980, we set out on our first full British tour, taking in Aylesbury Friars, Brighton and Cardiff and Sheffield Top Rank, Newcastle Mayfair, Derby Assembly Rooms, Cambridge Corn Exchange, East Anglia and Leicester University, Poole Arts Centre, Coventry Tiffany's, Stoke Hanley Victoria Hall, Swindon Brunel Rooms, Malvern Winter Gardens, Withernsea Grand Pavilion, Wakefield Unity Hall, Bristol and Portsmouth Locarno, Blackburn King George's Hall, Middleton Civic Hall, the Russell Club in Manchester, London's Hammersmith Palais, and finishing at the Top Rank in Birmingham. I was an avid reader of the *NME* and would try to read all our reviews. One of the best ones was written by Lynn Hanna, who picked up on my dancing in Leicester:

'Saxa forms the perfect foil for the childlike charm of The Beat's mercurial toaster. Ranking Roger's characteristic wide-brimmed hat makes him look fragile, like a bygone illustration of innocent youth. His elastic arms pump and his thin arms swing as he skips, skanks, and freezes in a dance stance at the front of the stage. …a dance beat that effortlessly fuses personal and political statements. If its basic function is escapist, it's also realistic multi-racial social comment that's optimistic just by virtue of what it is.'

Everyone in the band danced in their own unique way and jumped up and down because we had come through punk. Andy would do his funny wobbling legs movement, which I called the 'Elvis dance'. Dave had his own energy and David would play these weird, catchy bass lines and somehow twist his body out of time to them, which led to Saxa renaming him 'Shuffle': 'That's it, my man Shuffle.' We all laughed and it stuck. I tried singing and dancing out of time once and it was impossible. Shuffle could do it naturally. It's amazing but we rarely crashed into one another, although he did fall off stage once in America. It was a ten-foot fall. He shuffled off the stage and fell backwards. He was helped up by a roadie and with the balm of youthful adrenaline he carried on. Later he discovered a massive bruise on his torso. He was lucky and we had a good laugh about it afterwards.

Dancing was a vital ingredient of the 2 Tone concept and all the bands used to move about frenetically on stage. As infectious as the rhythms were for the audience, so they were for us, and I would put everything into a performance. Neville Staple was a big influence. I saw The Specials, and thought,

'Right, that's your job. You're Neville.' He would run and leap and climb anywhere he could on stage. Audiences loved it. I thought, 'Bloody hell! That's the way. If he can do that then I can too.' I'd never seen anything like it. As the front man you have to get the audience going. I knew what I had to do. Dancing released a lot of tension in audiences. We were aware of that and our intention was to give the audience a workout, so that by the end of the gig they would have to buy another T-shirt because they were soaking wet. It was fantastic to see an auditorium full and the audience on their feet; some fans would do the Madness dance, which I always thought looked a bit comic, but the most common dance was 'the skank'. It's defined in the dictionary:

'Skank/A noun. A steady-paced dance performed to reggae music, characterised by rhythmically bending forward, raising the knees, and extending the hands palms-downwards; (a piece of) reggae music suitable for such dancing.'

I would try to skank but over time it developed and I incorporated what I call 'the freeze', when I would literally freeze on stage in mid-movement. It was effective and unexpected. It was also my job to talk in-between songs. Dave would say, 'Come on Roge, say something to 'em.' I'd think, 'Shit. What do I say?' You'd find things to say: 'Are you happy? Do you want to dance? Are you still with us?' It would break it up and let people get their settings ready for the next song. By the end of a gig I would be exhausted. I still am. It's amazing how you can get through when you don't think you've got any energy. The audience and the vibes carry you. You shouldn't be in this business if you can't be bothered. If it's three people or three thousand I always put in the same effort. You never know who might be in an audience; one song in a movie can change the course of your whole life – the inclusion of 'March Of The Swivel Heads' in the Hollywood film *Ferris Bueller's Day Off* has paid me sufficient royalties to buy many luxuries, such as a nice car, and a home studio set-up – so I play every gig as if it's my first and last gig.

The scale of support for the band by now was growing at a rapid rate and with it came an increasing curiosity about us. In response, Andy's girlfriend – using the nom de plume Marilyn Hebrides – and Hunt Emerson launched a Beat fanzine called *The Noise In This World*. It offered fans a platform to share information and find out more about the band: tour news, record releases, lyrics, photographs, or simply, as Marilyn wrote in issue one, pass on useless pieces of information: 'Roger came into The Beat office in Handsworth sporting a new Police T-shirt (of which he's extremely proud) and with a few new phrases for you... SEEN, SIGHT UP. ROCKERS GALORE, MORE TIME STILL, which he proceeded to write all over the various pieces of paper I asked him to autograph.'

More important was a written feature called 'Gig Violence' about the continuing presence of British Movement skinheads at our concerts. 'I was at your gig at Brighton's Top Rank on Sunday,' wrote Rosalind, a fan from Falmer, Sussex, 'and

Me, 1981 © *Adrian Boot*

(Above) Saxa, Everett Morton,
David Steel, me, Dave Wakeling
and Andy Cox, circa 1981. © *Paul
Slattery/Retna/Photoshot*; (right)
with Joe Strummer © *Camera
Press/Paul Slattery*

(Above) me and
Saxa at the 'Jobs
For Youth' concert
in Bingley Hall,
November 24,
1981 © Andy (@
Birmingham_81)

(Clockwise from top) me and Saxa
at the 'Jobs For Youth' concert in
Bingley Hall, November 24, 1981
© Andy (@Birmingham_81); with
Rico Rodriguez, Ireland, 1981;
playing drums with Noel Redding,
Ireland.

(Clockwise from top) Everett
Morton, David Steele and Wesley
Magoogan on tour, 1982;
Andy Cox, US tour, 1982; Dave
'Blockhead' Wright, circa 1981.

(Left) onstage at
Tiffany's, Coventry,
1981 © *Syd Shelton*;
(above) **The Beat,
Coventry, 1981** © *Syd
Shelton*

(Above) The Beat
at the 'Save It For
Later' video shoot,
1982 © *Ziebra
Design*

enjoyed myself immensely, but one event spoiled the whole evening for me and for many people in your audience. You may already know that halfway through your set a wave of skinheads formed themselves into a solid line and pushed the crowd back against the wall chanting "Sieg Heil". What would have been a very grisly incident in fact dissolved into a few sporadic attacks against individuals – the isolated bloody violence that it seems people have come to expect since no one helped the guys getting their heads kicked in. There isn't a lot you can do about that, but I think as a band representing Peace and Unity, as you said, you could do something about the fascist thugs chanting Nazi slogans… in fact I didn't really think there was much you could do that would change them, but I was more concerned about the majority of your audience who were frightened and confused by the events.' Dave wrote a reply denouncing violence at gigs and adding, 'We sometimes feel that if we mention it on stage it sometimes gives the thugs a bigger buzz as it draws more attention to them and then the violence gets worse.'

Despite the unpleasant experience for some fans, the vast majority of our gigs were peaceful, joyous affairs and passed off without incident. Immediately after the British tour, we played our first gig overseas at the Hortens Festivalen in Norway. As we were driving through Scandinavia I remember being struck by the distance between people's houses. It seemed to suggest a model for humanity, in that humans need to have their own space. The festival headliners were Rick Wakeman and Billy

Cobham. It was all psychedelia and synthesisers and not our music or crowd. From Norway, we travelled to Germany to record our first European television show for *Rockpalast*, an equivalent of *The Old Grey Whistle Test*. The concert was filmed in front of a live audience but we soon settled any nerves and forgot about the cameras. There's footage of the concert online. It gives a good impression of what our set was and how we sounded in the summer of 1980. We played 'Pussy Price', 'Two Swords', 'Tears Of A Clown', 'Big Shot', 'Rough Rider', 'Best Friend', 'Can't Get Used To Losing You', 'Hands Off…She's Mine', 'Twist And Crawl', 'Whine And Grine/Stand Down Margaret', 'Ranking Full Stop', 'Mirror In The Bathroom', and for the encore, 'Click Click' and 'Jackpot'. The Beat were never as big in Germany as we were in the UK, or later in America. We did well in France and Holland but Germany was reserved, as you can see from the nonplussed audience.

I was sixteen when we signed our first record deal, which meant, as a minor, not only did Mum have to sign the contract on my behalf, I had to have a visa to travel to Europe. It was a legal requirement, so before we left the UK, John Mostyn would have to take me to Bow Street Magistrates Court to fill out the necessary documents, and on tour David 'Blockhead' Wright accepted the responsibility to be my guardian. I had to promise I wouldn't get into trouble, and by and large he let me do what I wanted. Thank God it was one of the musicians. Blockhead used to be a teacher and took the role very seriously. He did our lights, drove the van and also looked after Saxa to make sure he got his chicken every night. We liked him. He was educated and sensible. One day he was playing the keyboards and that was it, he joined us on stage and in time became a member of the band. I never told him, but he really reminded me of my old teacher, Mr O'Sullivan. Because of the kind of people The Beat were, I never got in trouble anyway. Those guys really changed me. I picked up so much by just watching their reactions and listening to how they talked. They were all very caring, patient people and slowly my cheeky little behaviours changed. I even began to question songs like 'Rough Rider'. I'd say, 'It's sexist. We can't do that.' They reasoned it was a sexy song and the woman was as happy as the man. 'He's not degrading her.' Well, that's the way I came to terms with it. Funnily enough, forty years later I had the same discussion with Pauline Black on our last tour!

After playing in Germany, we did a short tour of France supporting The Police, along with our old friends UB40, and Swindon's finest, XTC, who we had met on *Top of the Pops*. I have always credited The Police for paving the way for The Beat. They came in with the new wave thing a good year or two before 2 Tone exploded. I've often thought the title 'Message In A Bottle', and perhaps even 'Walking On The Moon', influenced Dave when he coined the phrase 'Mirror In The Bathroom'. Dave used similar-sounding words to Sting. But unlike The Beat, who were political from the outset, The Police weren't so until later on. We had things to say and I think Sting picked up on that from touring with us. By the time they released 'Spirits In The Material World' and 'Invisible Sun' about Northern Ireland, it was like, 'Hang on! Sting's getting political.' He realised The Police didn't have to be just a pop band and began writing more issue-based songs. If we had an effect I'm really pleased. After The Police split up in 1984, he wrote more overtly political songs like 'Russians' and 'We Work The Black Seam'. I followed his career, with an occasional walk-on part – more of which later – and would think, 'You're doing it, man.'

If I was to trace it back, Iggy Pop was one of the first artists to adopt a reggae rhythm and fuse it with a punk attitude. 'The Passenger' was an interpretation of reggae, particularly with the chopping guitar rhythm. Its impact was enormous on the underground scene and gave rise to many great songs, such as The Clash's 'Police And Thieves', Elvis Costello's 'Watching The Detectives', and even The Stranglers' 'Peaches', which perhaps didn't work as well. As I said before, The Beat came in at the right time. It was important that white people played reggae because, as a black person, I wanted to play punk. But if I'm honest, white people didn't play reggae as well as black players. I used to call it 'white reggae'. How do you define white reggae? 'C Moon' Paul McCartney. You couldn't play that at a dance. That changed when I heard Jim Brown from UB40. I never considered John Bradbury from The Specials a reggae drummer. He was a good rock drummer who could hold the reggae down and do the rim shot thing, but it was a different approach to Jim's. When you play reggae, everything is meant to be simplistic. There's hardly anything going on. One of the ways to recognise a great reggae drummer is by the drum fill. You'll hear the roll but not the cymbal crash at the end. The groove just sits back on the hi-hat. I'd give Brad a seven and Jim a ten.

I'm black British, but since I was born I've been listening to reggae music, and the same could be said for UB40. They grew up with songs like 'Red Red Wine' and 'Many Rivers To Cross' at blues dances. It was in their blood. They got to know and understand Jamaican rhythm and groove. Jim was the first white guy I saw play 'one drop', just like a Jamaican. I should explain: the basis of reggae is the 'one drop'. It's the heartbeat of reggae. If you're counting in four time – 1, 2, 3, 4 – the snare hits on the 2 and the 4. In reggae, the emphasis is on the 3. That's why it's called 'one drop'. The important thing is the kick and the snare are doing exactly the same thing at the same time on the 'one drop'. That's the power of reggae music. It's so simple; anything over it will sound powerful.

One of my favourite dub bands is called The Disciples. They're from England but I didn't discover that they were two white guys until years later. It proved to me that enjoying reggae had nothing to do with skin colour of the musicians. It comes from time and what you've been influenced by. I would never say 'white man hasn't got rhythm'. You can't say that because both white and black people have rhythm. I've seen brilliant white dancers. I've seen brilliant black dancers. Equally, I've seen white people who can't dance and black people who can't dance. I'm one of those black people who can't dance. All I do is jump around. But I'm having fun and enjoying myself. Everyone can see my joy and they join in. I'm saying, 'Come on everyone. Let's have a party.' That's my kind of dancing.

The first time The Beat played in Jamaica was for the World Music Festival. We stayed in the Rose Beach Country Club and Dave and I met up on the first night with Mick Jones and his then girlfriend, Daisy. We invited them to our room for a relaxing cigarette. There was a delay getting our key and when we finally got in the room there was someone else's clothes in there. Mick had brought a huge tape player with him and was blasting out some rap tracks that he had made in Paris and I was toasting over them. We ended up in the pool with Joe Jackson and listening to stories from The Clash's road crew. Our slot was on the Saturday evening and the experience was simultaneously hair raising and enlightening. It was the first time a Jamaican audience had seen an English black guy jumping up and down over rock music. We were playing a variation of their music in our style and I could sense their uncertainty – 'What's this all about?' But the songs went down great. 'Yeah man! The whites, them can play reggae. Them all right.' At the end we did an extended version of 'Tears Of A Clown' and the audience loved it. The following evening The Clash were due on at midnight but didn't get on stage until four-thirty in the morning, and a fight broke out between the band, their roadies, and the stage crew. Security wanted to pull the wire and cut their sound. The crowd loved it and the band played on. I learnt a lesson about The Clash that night: if one of them started something they all joined in and defended one another. They were like a family. Nobody touched their equipment. The Clash had had a raw ride in their early days so they had people to protect them. We had it easy by comparison.

During our European tour, I tried to keep out of the way of The Police, and I was conscious not to overstep my mark. Sting was a big star, and with his blonde hair and blue eyes was many a girl's heartthrob, but he always had time for me. It's not something you abuse. I saw him once lying on a grass strip reading a book and he called out to me. I was looking around to see where all of his bodyguards had gone and was pleasantly surprised to see him happy and relaxed in his own company. Sting ran five miles every day and a couple of mornings we jogged together. The first mile we would be side-by-side but I would struggle to keep up with his pace and he would sprint off. His minder was huge and I would have my work cut out just to keep ahead of him. I also got on really well with Stewart Copeland. He was always filming my toasting. During the tour we would have competitions to see who had the best weed. I'd come every day with something stronger just to outdo him. It was the same when I got to know The Clash: if you had good weed you were cool and part of the clan.

Every night, there was always one member of The Police checking out our show from the side of the stage, which I took as a huge compliment, but for me, hearing Stewart play every night was something else. He's a very clever fusion drummer and plays reggae his way. You only have to listen to 'Walking On The Moon', or 'Roxanne', with its back-to-front beat. I was obsessed with watching Stewart play. He is one of the best drummers I have ever seen. The Police may have had problems off stage but all of their anger and frustrations were released in the music. It made The Police. So many of their songs are classics and the noise they could make as a three-piece was brilliant.

When The Police reformed in 2007 to do a world tour I was as surprised as anybody. I hadn't seen them for years. They were due to play the National Indoor Arena in Birmingham so I went down in my car and found my way in during the soundcheck. I was working my way down from the top of the tiered seating and I could see them playing on stage. I didn't know whether to continue, and then one of their roadies spotted me and took me down to the stage. They were halfway through rehearsing a song and Sting stopped, and went, 'Hey Roger! Come here,' and gave me a big hug. Then he said, 'Obviously you're coming on with us tonight.' I was just wearing a tracksuit, so I said, 'Yeah, but I've got to go home and put some nice stage clothes on first and then I'll come straight back.' Sting said, 'Did you drive here?' I said, 'Yeah, I parked by the tour bus.' He said, 'Where are your keys?' I said, 'Here they are.' He snatched them off me, and said, 'Right, you're not going anywhere.' Then he turned to this other guy who worked for them, and said, 'Anything he wants…' I had a slap-up meal.

The gig was fantastic. I went on for 'Roxanne'. I had no idea what I was going to do. Sting introduced me: 'Ladies and gentlemen here's Birmingham's own Ranking Roger.' There was a big cheer and I just thought, 'You've got to go for it, boy.' And freestyled. There's something about catching a moment with an audience. You have to egg them on. At first they sing quietly and then you shout, 'Louder,' and you can hear nervous giggles. I've always been adept at cajoling audiences and getting them involved. It's what I'm good at but I don't know how I do it. All I know is that if I'm put on the spot and there's fire under my feet I can get them. That's what my talent is.

'Roxanne' was the last number but as I left the stage Sting grabbed my arm, and said, 'Stay. We're all going to bow.' Stewart came out from behind the kit and somehow as we bent over I caught Andy Summers in the eye with the nail on my little finger. It was completely unintentional but he stormed off and backstage went absolutely mad. I went up to him to try and apologise but he didn't want to know. He kind of just walked off as I was trying to talk to him. I thought, 'I haven't got time for this. Leave it.' Unlike Stewart, who was a gentleman and very humble, and Sting, who was a very spiritual person – interested in *The Urantia Book* and very different from how you see him on television – Andy was always in his own world.

Stop Your Sobbing

**Pretenders. Special Beat. Talking Heads.
Specials in Ireland**

As I said earlier, 'Stand Down Margaret' was unofficially banned on daytime radio and as a result we noticed our gigs in the UK started to go downhill. Luck intervened when The Pretenders and Talking Heads both said, 'Come to the States and play with us.' Madness, The Specials and The Selecter had all been to America, and Steel Pulse had opened up for The Police. I kept on hearing about New York. I was dying to get there. On September 3, 1980, we travelled down to the BBC's Maida Vale studios and recorded four new songs for a Radio 1 John Peel Session – 'Too Nice To Talk To', 'Walk Away', 'Monkey Murders' and 'New Psychedelic Rockers'. The next day, we flew out to Cleveland, Ohio, to support The Pretenders on seventeen dates.

After the first gig, Chrissie Hynde and I got talking over dinner. She was saying, 'Good show.' I was charmed: 'Wow!

The star has spoken to me.' The next couple of dates were in Chicago and Illinois. The audience didn't know who The Beat were but we went down really well, which I think was down to 'Tears Of A Clown'. It was a classic and people always wanted to sing and dance along to it. The Pretenders were getting all the radio play because of their hits 'Brass In Pocket' and 'Stop Your Sobbing', but we were blowing them off stage. They didn't like it. After the third gig, their soundchecks began to take longer or would suspiciously start later. We then stopped getting soundchecks altogether. They did everything to make sure we had half the lights, half the PA sound level, and people who got up to dance were sometimes thrown out during our second or third number. It was very disheartening. It was The Pretenders' gig and our job was to warm up the audience, so we had to be humble, but we all thought, 'We'll never play with them again.' We could have been friends and worked together, but, 'Thank you, but we don't need that.' I might be wrong but that's how it felt. Inwardly, it made us more resilient: 'Let's fight like lions. Take no prisoners.' It was weird. I don't hold anything against the band and I'm not sure The Pretenders were even aware of it. But that is how the music business worked in the early Eighties; in those days, if you were a support band, you were thankful to get a soundcheck.

Despite our ongoing resentments, the tour continued on through Kansas City, St Louis, Memphis, Atlanta, Richmond, Virginia Beach, Washington, Baltimore, New

Haven and New York. One of my abiding memories was when we played in the south. We all got out of the bus at a truck stop – dressed totally different, different ages, black and white – and they were like, 'Are you a table tennis team?' Obviously you heard stories about lynchings in the south and the Ku Klux Klan, but we didn't confront any racism. Nobody came up to you, like they did in England, and said, 'You black bastard.' The prejudice was hidden beneath the surface and I definitely sensed uncomfortableness with certain promoters and security staff. People just weren't used to seeing black and white musicians together. I remember going into a bar and the place went quiet. I asked for an orange juice and the whole atmosphere suddenly changed. 'Are you from out of town? Are you from England?' If I had been a local it would have been, 'Get out of here, boy.' When we played at the University of Alabama in 1982, the mayor decreed November 29 as 'English Beat in Birmingham day', and issued a signed proclamation franked with a wax seal of the city. Jumping ahead again, when I toured the States with Special Beat in the early Nineties, a police officer came backstage to talk with me and Neville. He was curious about us and ended up taking both of us for a spin in his patrol car. The next time we came to town he took us to meet his family. It was like we were his trophies. He could hold us up, and say, 'Look. These black guys aren't so bad after all.' As an English black man in America, curiosity will make people listen, whereas for an American black man it would have been a whole lot harder.

On September 23 we arrived in New York, where we stayed at the Empire Hotel on 44 West 63rd Street. I remember the hotel because it had thick bulletproof doors. I thought, 'It must be proper Gangsterville round here.' Instead of going out to explore I went to my room and locked myself in. The following day, the tour manager talked me into going out for a walk. As soon as I stepped outside it was hectic and heavy. New York got on top of me; all the big massive buildings. I couldn't take it. Everything was too fast. We did two nights at the Ritz and the Palladium and then after playing final dates in New Jersey, Boston and Pennsylvania we had a week off.

On April 14, 1983, two years after we had supported The Pretenders, their bass player, Pete Farndon, drowned at home in his bath from a heroin overdose. I liked Pete a lot. He had all the time in the world for you. And then on April 16, two days after Pete, James Honeyman-Scott, the guitar player, died of a heart failure caused by excessive cocaine. It was a great shame and marked the end of an era for The Pretenders. Over time, Chrissie Hynde recruited new members, and I admired her for keeping the band going and having more chart success with songs like 'Don't Get Me Wrong' and 'Hymn To Her'. It's great to still see a regrouped Pretenders out on the live circuit today and making new records.

While we were in the States, filmmaker Joe Massot had been travelling around the UK shooting footage of all the 2 Tone bands, including Bad Manners, who were seen as part of the whole ska revival. The film crew flew out to join us in

Emerald City, Cherry Hall, New Jersey, to record our set. It was a great gig and we finished off by playing 'Click Click' and 'Jackpot' as an encore, but the audience kept on clapping and shouting for more. We had already played for an hour, so for a second time we went back on and played 'Big Shot' and 'Twist And Crawl'. We were all saying, 'Great! We're going to be in a movie.' But when I saw *Dance Craze*, the finished film, I was disappointed. It could have been much better. There was no story or backstage action or interviews. An album was released the following year with a live soundtrack featuring three of our songs – 'Mirror In The Bathroom', 'Big Shot' and 'Ranking Full Stop' – and two additional songs could be seen in the film: 'Rough Rider' and 'Twist And Crawl'. In its defence, *Dance Craze* is the only visual archive of all the 2 Tone bands together, and to a degree, it captures the energy of the movement shortly before it began to wane.

While we were touring in America we came across some mods and rude boys but very few of them understood what 2 Tone was about. We had to explain to them what ska and reggae was and how, as a band, we had evolved as much out of new wave, which after punk was big in the States. People would say, 'Oh, it wasn't Sting who invented this music then?' We'd say, 'No! Listen to Bob Marley sing *ee yo yo yo*. Sting got a lot of licks from The Wailers.' He used it smartly and it sounded great.

A decade later, in the early Nineties, there was the so-called 'third wave of ska' in the States. They got it so wrong.

It was a funky, heavy metal style with an offbeat and they called it ska. Their influence may have been 2 Tone but they sounded nothing like us. I guess by the same token, The Skatalites would have said the same about us and The Specials not sounding anything like original Jamaican ska. During the 'third wave of ska' I joined forces with Neville Staple, from The Specials, and we formed Special Beat. No Doubt opened up for us. We offered them the whole tour but they could only afford to do the West Coast. We were all after their singer Gwen Stefani but she remained loyal to her boyfriend, No Doubt's bass player, Tony Kanal.

Special Beat was a fifty-fifty mix of Specials and Beat songs. The gigs were amazing and we toured across America and then on to Europe and the UK. It could have gone really far, but it wasn't very well coordinated. Still, Special Beat was one of the best live outfits I've ever been in. They used to call me and Neville 'double turbo'. We really got the crowd going. It was chaos on the stage. We were always bashing into each other trying to outdo each other to see who was the fittest. Neville won hands down; he had enormous stomach muscles. The audience reaction was phenomenal and at some gigs I thought the roof would explode with the vibe we were giving out. It was a very 'special' time.

Special Beat did a tour with Sting on the *Soul Cages* tour and each night he would ask us to come on stage for the encore and do 'Walking On The Moon', 'Every Breath You Take' and 'Message In A Bottle'. One night, Sting's wife, Trudie, asked me to teach her how to skank at the side of the stage. She was really pleased when she got it. Neville and I kept Special Beat going for about two and a half years and then I fell out with Lynval Golding, who was playing guitar with us. We'd sit down and make a plan and then Lynval would change it. After a while it really began to get on my nerves. If we were on Plan A, Lynval would be on Plan D, so I split the band up. We'd been on the road a good couple of months and tensions had slowly built up. Maybe certain people were drinking or taking cocaine – I don't do either – but we were singing all these songs about love and unity. We came to the last song, 'Jackpot', and mid-song I said to myself, 'Where have the drums gone?' I looked back and saw Lynval with his guitar high in the air about to whack Brad on his head. I said, 'OI! WHAT DO YOU THINK YOU'RE DOING? THIS BAND'S ALL ABOUT LOVE AND UNITY. YOU'RE FUCKING UP THE WHOLE THING.' I dropped my mic, walked off stage, and that was the end of Special Beat. I didn't want to know after that. Lynval's behaviour went against all my beliefs. You address issues in the dressing room away from the public and you reason them out. I couldn't believe what I had seen. I knew Brad and Lynval had been getting on each other's nerves – Brad used to drink a lot and then he would change. When he was sober he was the nicest man in the world, and often the next day, I'd tell him what he had been like and he'd say he couldn't remember. He'd say, 'Really? Did I do that? I'm so sorry, Roger.' And he would

144

mean it. I've seen drink and drugs destroy so many people. All the 2 Tone bands took cocaine. But I grew up on roots music and the message within that was the warning not to go that way.

In 2009, I was persuaded to reform Special Beat to celebrate the thirtieth anniversary of 2 Tone. We were called The Legends of Ska and did a tour of Australia, inviting Pauline Black to join us. She would go on first and do six Selecter songs, then Neville would do six Specials songs and I would finish with six Beat songs. It worked really well, but during the tour Neville's mood declined and he became suicidal. I went to his hotel room one night because I was so concerned. He was pulling his hair out and cussing the original Specials because they wanted to reform and he didn't. I was saying, 'Neville, you have to do it.' He was saying, 'They're full of bullshit.' Neville spent years slagging his former bandmates off; even when The Specials were originally together they were constantly at each other's throats. I would say to Neville, 'It's your legacy. Use it.' I tried to calm him down, but all the time there seemed to be something more than The Specials worrying him, but I couldn't put my finger on what it was. He didn't seem like the Neville of old. I stayed with him for a couple of hours and then I went to bed. The next morning the band was having breakfast and Neville bounded in all happy-go-lucky. I didn't click the reason behind the abrupt mood change until one of the crew whispered to me, 'Could be he's just scored some crack, don't you think?'

* * *

Back to September, 1980: after The Pretenders' attempts at disrupting our support slot it was a great relief to join Talking Heads on tour. That was until we sabotaged our own show. The first gig was at the Greek Theatre in Los Angeles and we were due to go on stage at eight o'clock. Plenty of time we thought, so Dave Peters, the sound engineer, Shuffle, Everett and I decided to go for a day trip to Disneyland. It was a sixty-mile round trip and we arrived at the theme park in good time. We had a ball even though you had to queue up for hours for a ride that only lasted two minutes. It was school-boy fun; Shuffle and I kept tapping Mickey Mouse on the back and when he turned round we'd freeze and try not to laugh. Shuffle was usually quiet but we could still have a laugh. I may as well at this point share a piece of useless information: Shuffle used to hate egg yolks and I used to hate egg whites, so we'd swap them between us.

By mid-afternoon we sensibly left Disneyland and immediately hit traffic. We were at a virtual standstill for the whole journey back to the venue. When we finally arrived, we were rushed backstage only to be informed that it was now exactly the time we were due to finish our set. We were devastated. 'Oh my God! That's it. They won't have us on tour now. We've fucked it.' We were a bag of nerves. David Byrne came over and laughed it off: 'Is everyone all right? Don't worry about it. There's always tomorrow.' He could have been really arrogant and instead found the whole story hilarious. It was so nice of him. Tina Weymouth also gave us a big hug: 'You poor guys.' I was like, 'Wow!' I thought I'd be in trouble. The next day we got more publicity for missing the gig than playing it. The following night was fantastic. We got a standing ovation and Sylvie Simmons reported in *Sounds* 'openers just don't *do* encores at the Greek Theatre'.

David Byrne was down to earth and didn't have any airs and graces, and I spent a lot of time with Tina and Chris Frantz. They were the pranksters. Talking Heads was a brilliant band. They were promoting *Remain In Light*, which had been produced by Brian Eno, and they were experimenting with African sounds and refreshing funk rhythms. We used to listen to them on the bus. The band liked a lot of the same music and increasingly we brought African rhythms into our sound. You can hear a West African highlife influence on 'Too Nice To Talk To', which was written on that tour.

I would record the band jamming in rehearsal to take home and listen to and get vibes from. Frequently I would hear ideas and think, 'That could be a tune. Why don't we use that?' That's how 'Too Nice To Talk To' came about. Everett and Shuffle had been playing the rhythm in soundcheck during the Talking Heads tour. 'Oh, they're doing that groove again.' BOOF! All of a sudden it became a song. We recorded it once we got back to England and released it as a stand-alone single in December 1980. It spent eleven weeks on the chart and reached number seven in the second week of January 1981. By this point, Madness were enjoying a fantastic run of success since leaving 2 Tone with consecutive hit singles – 'One Step

Beyond', 'My Girl', 'Night Boat To Cairo', 'Baggy Trousers' and 'Embarrassment' – and when we performed 'Too Nice To Talk To' on *Top of the Pops*, Chas, Bedders and Chrissy Boy jumped on stage during the recording and started dancing and messing about behind us. You might imagine that we knew all the bands on 2 Tone, but the first time I properly met Madness was in 1984 when they invited me and Dave to sing on a couple of tracks for their fifth album, *Keep Moving*. We went to their studio for one day, learnt two songs – 'Victoria Gardens' and 'Waltz Into Mischief' – and added some vocals. Suggs was there but sadly I've never met him or Madness since.

The second time we performed 'Too Nice To Talk To' on *Top of the Pops*, Dave dressed in a Soviet army uniform complete with CND badge. It was cool and reflected the military costumes we were wearing on stage. By coincidence, The Specials were plugging their latest single, 'Do Nothing', on the same show and we decided to swap bass players for the recording. Consequently, and unknown to the BBC, Horace played with The Beat and Shuffle took to the stage with The Specials. We were miming so it didn't matter what notes they were playing but I think Horace learnt Shuffle's part in the dressing room during the rehearsal. The two of them looked quite similar and we got one over on the BBC. Musicians 1, *Top of the Pops* 0.

We had only played once before with The Specials and during *Top of the Pops* we hatched a plan to do a short tour together. Two months later we set off for Ireland. It was absolutely brilliant. We did four dates and all travelled together on a tour coach. At first, The Beat sat at the back and The Specials were in the middle and up front, but we soon mingled. I got on with everyone. Both bands were realists and very much the opposite of pop stars. I was on tour with one of my favourite bands and although I always felt The Specials were bigger than us, we alternated the headline. It was a great idea. The bands were evenly matched. It worked really well and created a mutual respect between us. There wasn't a hierarchy but we soon discovered it was harder to follow The Specials, and headline.

When Rico and Saxa met you couldn't stop them. They were vibing about people and places in Jamaica and I remember thinking, 'It's caught fire, here.' It wasn't unusual for Saxa to stay on stage at the end of a gig and do an encore. He'd blow for five minutes or play 'Stranger On The Shore' and then we'd all come out and join him. When Rico and Saxa played together it was a great jam. I was tremendously sad when they both passed away but people say, 'Rico and Saxa are now in the 2 Tone orchestra up in the sky with Brad from The Specials.'

The first gig at Ulster Hall in Belfast had been organised as a benefit for Carri Melo, an interdenominational group who provided holidays on the West Coast of Ireland for deprived children. The gig raised over £2,000. Inside the venue the atmosphere was electric. We hadn't realised how much the fans wanted to see us. They were starved of music. We were the biggest thing since bloody Jimi Hendrix as far as they were concerned. Before we went on stage I walked through the audience to get a feel for the mood, and a skinhead came up to me and spat in my ear. I called security and they dragged him out. I realised after that he'd only pretended to spit, but still, it wasn't a nice gesture. Some of his mates came over, and were saying, 'Ignore him. He's stupid. We've come to enjoy ourselves.' While we were talking, it dawned on me they were all Protestants. They said, 'That'll be because all the Catholics have to sit upstairs.' I didn't like it. It would have been the equivalent of separating black and white people at a gig. During our set there was a lot of shouting and I could see Catholic kids flicking cigarette butts over the top of the balcony on to the Protestants below. Dave said he saw people pissing over the balcony but I don't remember that. Fortunately, there wasn't any trouble. I remember saying to the audience, 'People need to learn to live in love and unity. This is what Beat music is all about.' Maybe we had an effect on those people. I hope we did.

We stayed in the Europa, which was infamous as the most bombed hotel in Belfast. It had barbed wire around the perimeter and was patrolled by armed police. The entrance had a metal detector. When we arrived there were about fifteen or twenty fans outside behind the gate. They all knew that's where bands stayed. I went to talk with them and signed some autographs. There was a mix of Catholic and Protestants but there was no animosity between them. I was trying to get them to talk and naturally they wanted to know what religion I was. I said that I had been brought up Catholic and one of them cheered. The others frowned. 'But it doesn't matter,' I said, 'because we all believe in God.'

The following day we played the Stardust Ballroom in Dublin. The place was heaving. It was too packed. We went on first and went down a storm. Towards the end of the set some kids started doing Nazi salutes but there wasn't any real trouble. The Specials came on and launched into 'Concrete Jungle', and fights broke out down the front. I was told later that the trouble was between two rival gangs in the audience, the Coolock Boot Boys and the Edenmore Dragons from Raheny. During 'Gangsters', The Specials had to stop playing. Terry was saying, 'We hate violence.' Security got it under control but then during 'Sock It To 'Em JB', part of the PA system, on the left-hand side, fell down and just missed a whole cluster of kids. You could see it was going to happen all night. There were too many people, pushing and shoving forward. Neville shouted, 'I told you so.' It was chaos. Fights were breaking out and then all hell broke loose when skinheads got on the stage and started breaking all the gear up; drums were flying everywhere. I thought, 'I need to get out of here, man.' I made my way to the back of the stage with a roadie and we tried to break open the exit doors but they had been padlocked. I tried a martial arts kick but I couldn't break the chains. I was kicking full brute but we couldn't unlock them.

I was thinking, 'Shit'. The next thing we knew, skinheads had got backstage and there were fights breaking out in our dressing room. We ended up barricading ourselves in an adjacent room with sofas pushed up against the door. Eventually, the trouble died down and we came out; there was blood up the walls and broken glass everywhere.

A month later the Stardust burnt down. Some say it was an electrical fault but after a trial, a verdict of arson was returned. My heart goes out to the forty-eight people who died that night. People tried to escape through the fire exits but were thwarted by the padlocked doors. Christy Moore was prosecuted for writing a song called 'They Never Came Home', which included a line about hundreds of children being injured due to chained fire exits. That could have been us. It was a lucky escape. I guess it wasn't our turn.

From Dublin, we crossed over to west Ireland, where the arrival of The Beat and The Specials was big news. We played at the Leisureland, Galway, and then UCC Downtown Kampus in Cork. Fans were saying, 'Thank you very much. Nobody ever comes to play for us.' The whole city was there. My girlfriend's parents lived in Cork and they both came to the gig. I'd met Angela's mother before but not her father. Angela – and Dominique, who was Dave's girlfriend – did wardrobe for The Beat, so they were on tour with us. It was good to have women with us. It changed the atmosphere and curbed any sexism.

I had known Angela since school. We were in the same year as each other. I had fancied her big time when I was thirteen but she wasn't interested. I asked her out several times and she always turned me down. Eventually, I wore her down, and she said yes. We went out with each other for two years and then she went back to Ireland when we were in the fourth year. I went to see her off at the airport and I was crying because I thought we would never see each other again. We stayed in touch for a while but then Angela moved house again and our relationship fizzled out. A couple of years later, I was with a couple of girlfriends in Birmingham going for a night out in town. One of the girls said, 'Let's have a drink, first.' We walked into the local pub – 'Tears Of A Clown' was out so I was immediately recognised – and somebody came over, and said to me, 'Hey Roger, did you know Angela's back? She's over there.' 'WHAT!' I couldn't believe it. I was really excited. I said, 'Excuse me, ladies,' and went over to Angela and we started talking. After a while, the girls came over and said, 'Are you coming?' I said, 'I need to stay.' I thought, 'If I go now I'll never get the chance again.' That night my life changed forever.

Angela and I carried on talking but she was unsure about going out with me again. Two years is a long time, at that age, and neither of us were kids anymore. I was saying, 'I've changed. I'm not the same as I was at school.' Her brother Michael was there and talked her into giving it a go. He said, 'Roger's all right, you know.' Finally, Angela said, 'All right. I'll give it a chance.' We fell in love with each other and it was fantastic. From that moment I never let her leave my sight.

153

But when her dad found out, he wasn't pleased to say the least. Her mum was English and he was Irish; he didn't want his daughter going out with a black man and stopped Angela seeing me. At the time, Angela was living with her Auntie Eileen, a ten-minute walk from my house. Eileen adored me and was a good woman. I could reason with her about anything under the sun. She was open-minded and allowed Angela and I to see each other. It was a love that was unstoppable.

When The Beat and The Specials arrived at the venue in Cork, Angela's parents were there. I was scared to meet her dad but we shook hands. And he was great. After the gig, I stayed at their house so they could get to know me. I wanted to show that I loved their daughter. They knew I was a pop star and they saw all the women screaming at the gig, so they were justifiably concerned. It could have been nasty but I never considered Angela's father to be racist. There were many Irish parents who had forbidden their daughters from going out with a black man. It was fear of the unknown. Before Angela, I had many white girlfriends. Mum didn't mind. Like me, she didn't see colour. She wasn't prejudiced like other Caribbean people. Being brought up in a house full of women made me see life differently. I think in stereo, not mono. There are many ways to deal with a situation. Around 1978, all of a sudden it seemed like white women had decided that black men were flavour of the month. It was the first time I saw black men and white women having relationships and having kids together. By the Eighties it felt acceptable. The horror of 'they're going to take over the country' seemed to pass and by the Nineties the racism aimed at black people was directed at Kosovans and then the Poles. Newcomers are always scapegoated.

As a final note, at the end of the tour, when The Specials left Ireland, there was an incident at the airport. Horace wrote in his book *Ska'd For Life* that customs confiscated £8,000, raised from the tour, on the grounds that it contravened Irish currency laws. Horace says the money was returned fifteen years later and divided up amongst the band. He bought a new sofa. I had no idea and we certainly never benefitted from the unexpected dividend. Wait till I see them Specials!

A Quick Burn With The Beat

Wha'ppen? Hit It

We had spent six weeks making the first album. Then we spent nine months promoting it around Europe and America. All of a sudden the record company said, 'Right, it's time for a new album.' We had been playing a lot of new songs and knew what we wanted to record. And so, on February 25, 1981, we decamped to London for six weeks to make our second album, *Wha'ppen?* Where you record can dictate how an album ends up sounding. We stayed in Harrowby Court, Marylebone, in a cushioned, relaxed environment, and whereas the first album was the raw sound of The Beat, the new songs were chilled and restful. People were saying, 'It's more laid-back. You've gone for the "one-drop" instead of the four on the square.'

Before we went into the studio we received a letter from a gym instructor in California, who told us how she had been trying to get her class to do dance steps to our record but it was too fast. She wrote, 'Call yourself dance music... you should slow it down a bit.' We never met the woman but we took note. In fact, we tentatively planned to call the record *Dance Yourself Stupid* to reflect the effects of dancing and the optimism and goodness it generated in an audience's soul. It was one of many alternative titles considered, which included *Insect*, *Motion Lotion*, *Human Racing*, *The Unrest Cure*, and *Misdemean*, which was a combination of 'Mr Mean' and 'misdemeanour'. We settled on *A Quick Burn With The Beat*, for which Hunt designed an 'identikit' front cover of all the band members rolled into one. Apparently it looked like Terry Hall. At the last minute the title changed to *Wha'ppen?*, which was a greeting amongst the band and our catchphrase. We told Hunt that we wanted a cartoonish picture of the band with a psychedelic tidal wave behind us about to strike and take us away. Somebody would then say, 'Wha'ppen?' The back cover features studio snaps from when we were on tour and travelled along the west coast of France with The Police. One day we went on the beach and covered each other in sand. Blockhead whipped out a camera and took a photograph of me buried up to my chest. There's a picture from the time Andy was tied up with rope. As a point of trivia, our title for the first album was almost *Compulsion* before we opted for *I Just Can't Stop It*.

Recording at the Roundhouse again, we would go to the studio at about ten or eleven in the morning and work through to the end of the day, invariably into the early hours. I recorded my vocals after all the backing tracks had been recorded but I went to the studio most days. I enjoyed hearing and watching what was being recorded. I can't read music but I can tell you when something doesn't sound right. I would hear melodies and make suggestions or point out mistakes. I was another ear adding ideas. My duty was to put people right, particularly about how to play reggae. When I first joined the band they were doing a lot of things wrong. I was always suggesting ideas. I'd say to Everett, 'Just keep that beat. No crashes.' We would all work together. It was like, 'Try putting this note there or change it to this.' I'd say to Shuffle, 'Hold the bass line. You can do all the tricky stuff but keep the same line for the groove. Let it go round.' He would be quite happy to incorporate an idea if he thought it would work. You tried it and if it worked you stuck to it. It was the same with the guitars. I didn't think the offbeat guitar sounded like proper reggae. I'd say, 'This is how you do it. Dampen the chord like this.' Small changes made a big difference. I saw myself as a vibes man. When it was manic and there was enough echo and dub I was happy.

Dave was a clever lyricist. As I wrote earlier, I would hand ideas to him or toast things, and he'd say, 'Why don't you try saying that word instead?' He was good with words and would help me. Even though I held my own, Dave was on another level of writing. I learnt a lot of my strategy through him. I would be writing and the others would throw a line in and we'd all laugh, 'Yeah, go on. Let's put it in.' 'Psychedelic Rockers' was like that. We just wanted something different and a bit trippy and not to sound like other toasting out there. Dave said, 'Try this and see what happens.'

At the edge of your nerves where the lights are pretty
A change in the weather as it smothers the city
Psychedelic, psychedelic

'Psychedelic Rockers' was about an atomic bomb and the fear of nuclear annihilation. A similar theme was present in 'I Am Your Flag', which was a track we donated to the compilation album *Life In The European Theatre*. The record had been organised by John Mostyn and our former tour manager, Chas Mervyn. The album featured the cream of British music – The Clash, The Jam, The Specials, Madness, XTC, Ian Dury, Peter Gabriel, Bad Manners, The Stranglers, The Undertones, Echo & The Bunnymen, the Au Pairs – and the royalties from the record's sales were allocated to anti-nuclear campaigns and Friends of the Earth. Dave wrote 'I Am Your Flag' about young working-class men being used to fight in the name of nationalism *dying to become a man because I am your flag*. While we had been on tour in America, we were struck by how proud people were of their flag. You would see the Stars & Stripes everywhere. If you saw that many Union Jacks in England, you'd think 'National Front'.

'Soleil Trop Chaud' came from a song the band were playing, and I said, 'That sounds like an old St Lucian tune,' so I started singing *c'est chaud, soleil trop chaud*, which translated is simply *it's too hot, the sun is too hot*. They said, 'Yeah! Go on. That sounds great, whatever you're singing.' The version I knew was from a 1974 cadence-lypso record by Les Grammacks, which my parents had. Jefferson Joseph, who was from Dominica, wrote it. I can't speak French, but I understood Mum when she used to cuss me in St Lucian patois, so I got to know it really well. The others listened to the original, I toasted over the chords they had been jamming and we added the title 'French Toast'. During the take, Saxa shouted 'Wow! What a sound. Dig it man,' and we kept it in. If you listen closely around two minutes into the song you'll hear the man's delight. The song was a departure for The Beat and again reflected the band's African listening tastes.

Wha'ppen? was an eclectic album. It went from 'Doors Of Your Heart' to 'French Toast (Soleil Trop Chaud)' to 'Get-A-Job', about unemployment, which was more in the spirit of the first album. Cedric Myton sang backing vocals on 'Doors Of Your Heart' as a thank you from us after we put out *Heart Of The Congos* on Go Feet. The Congos were formed in 1976 by Cedric, Roy Johnson and Watty Burnett and they recorded *Heart Of The Congos* on an 8-track the following year working with producer Lee Perry at his Black Ark studio. Three different mixes of the album were made, and ahead of giving it its first ever UK release on Go Feet, we had the record cleaned up, recut, and re-pressed from the original masters. They were thrilled to have it available for the first time in the UK. It sold really well for a Jamaican reggae record. We released a second album, *Face The Music* by Cedric Myton & The Congos, which included contributions from Rico and Dick from The Specials. Cedric had the voice of an angel. He could reach those high tones and his voice would stay soft and full. We became good friends with him but we ended up giving him a lot of money because I think he saw us as the record company. He would say, 'Someone is sick in Jamaica...' If I had doubts about where the money was going they were appeased by his skill in the kitchen. Cedric cooked some of the best food I have ever tasted in my life. His speciality was seafood. He was like a world class chef. It's probably the secret behind his beautiful backing vocals on 'Doors Of Your Heart'.

I wrote the toast in 'Doors Of Your Heart' in the studio while the song was being recorded. I thought, 'This is about love of the heart and I'm about "love of the people".' I was looking to say something that other toasters hadn't done before, so I wrote about love and unity and complemented *love thumping* and the heart going *pump pump* and beating faster:

This one your Unity Rocker, Lord
Stick him in your living room and turn off the light eh!
Bet you wouldn't know if he was black or white, boy!
Say what's the use in fighting
Man say, I say you shouldn't really fight.
Take him to a discotheque and take him to a pub
Take him to a blues and then you play him a rub-a-dub, ehhh!

Man say you shouldn't really fight.
Each and every day I walk through the streets and I see man
a man want kill each other
'cos you are black or you are white.
So what's the use in fighting?

The video for 'Doors Of Your Heart' was a combination of real footage from the Notting Hill Carnival and our own set-up to make it look like we were there. It was directed by Julien Temple, who had directed *The Great Rock 'n' Roll Swindle* and would later direct the video for 'Save It For Later'. I liked his style. Julien filmed us playing on the back of a lorry and in a rooftop garden but the greatest challenge was the toast section. An authentic-looking sound system had been built under the Westway and loads of black people started hanging around to see what was happening. I had spent three years playing in front of predominantly white people and suddenly it was a majority black audience. Thank God it was a slow tune and not a fast toast. And even though I was only miming I felt enormous pressure to win over the crowd. My moves had to look good and for a moment I was really hesitant. In the end I played it cool. At the end of the MC, Julien suggested I should swing on a rope. I was thinking, 'What! You think I'm monkey man or something?' But it worked and I swung off the makeshift stage, over the crowd, and out of shot. The video came out really well.

During the album recording, *The Face* made contact and invited me to do a front cover feature. I felt privileged to be asked. *The Face* was a new fashion, culture and music magazine and was striking for its visual imagery. It launched in 1980 with a front cover photograph of Jerry Dammers. On the day of the shoot they asked if I would wear a zoot suit and hold a saxophone, despite the fact that I had never played one in my life. I tried on the zoot suit and it looked good. I had wanted to find my own niche to move away from the rude boy image. The Beat never dressed uniformly like the other 2 Tone bands and when we performed 'All Out To Get You' on *Top of the Pops* our individual styles were clearly evident: I wore a new double-breasted zoot suit with a waistcoat, and I seem to remember two Japanese girls helped me to dress; Dave wore a new double-breasted grey suit; Shuffle a Charles and Diana wedding T-shirt; Everett a *More Specials* T-shirt with the slogan 'I'm just a stereotype', and Andy looked like a hippie in a loose-fitting yellow ethnic shirt. Fashion was carrying us forward. A fortnight before, we had performed 'Drowning' on *Top of the Pops*, and if you watch the footage closely, Saxa is playing a tenor sax instead of the recorded alto sax part because he thought we were there to play 'All Out To Get You'. In the dressing room, beforehand, he had to work out the different fingering a tenor sax requires. Peter Powell introduced us, and said, 'One of the very best cuts of vinyl you can get in the shops at the moment has got to be this. It's a double A-side from The Beat. They've got "All Out To Get You" on one and this, by far my favourite. It's called "Drowning". Just hear this.'

'Drowning' was a song Dave had written in a toilet in New York while we were on tour with The Pretenders the previous year. He was hiding in the cubicles because he was disenchanted with the record company and didn't want to go out for dinner with them. Dave said that he felt like he was drowning and that gave him the impetus for the lyrics. Apparently, by turning down the label's invitation he missed the opportunity to meet Freddie Mercury. Nevertheless, 'Drowning' had a fantastic bass line; it was when Shuffle mastered reggae. In the studio, Andy added garden shears to the track for percussive effect, which Bob added a backwards effect to, to enhance the sound. The accompanying video was shot in a swimming pool. Everett couldn't swim so he stayed in the shallow end. I hated it. But I guess it was different.

Filming at the BBC usually took all day, and while I was wandering around the building I met Phil Lynott from Thin Lizzy. There was a corridor with artists' names by the side of the doors and Phil's door was open. I popped my head in, and he said, 'All right mate.' He was so friendly. I'd never met him before but I went in, and said, 'I'm Roger from The Beat. I've listened to your music for years.' Phil Lynott was not only black, but he was from Ireland and was hugely successful. I was thinking, 'I wonder what his story is?' I shook his hand, and he said, 'I really like your music, man.' I was like: 'Wow!' He was taller than me and had big hands. The old rockers are the best.

In May, we set out on a British tour to promote the release of *Wha'ppen?* I liked the new album but I've always felt that *I Just Can't Stop It* is the best Beat album. That's the classic one and has a lot of our naïve hunger captured in the music. Whereas *Wha'ppen?* made you move your hips, *I Just Can't Stop It* made you move your feet. The band was growing and we tried to change too quickly. The album lacked diversity. I didn't like all of the songs. In part, it was too same-ish, particularly in the drumming patterns. The difference between the first two Beat records is much like the difference between The Specials' records. *Specials* is the raw fusion of ska and punk and *More Specials* is more experimental, with weird Spanish and muzak influences and songs like 'International Jet Set' and 'Stereotype'.

To replicate the expanded sound on *Wha'ppen?*, we took a trumpet player, Eddie Saltin, who was a friend of Saxa's, and Cedric Myton on tour with us, taking in Cardiff, Bristol, Nottingham, Leicester, Aylesbury, Hanley, Birmingham, Lancaster, Leeds, Glasgow, Edinburgh, Manchester, Liverpool, Wolverhampton, Gloucester, Portsmouth, St Austell and finishing with two London dates at the Rainbow and the Hammersmith Palais, with Linton Kwesi Johnson opening for us. We tried to keep ticket prices affordable at £3.50, or £2.50 on production of a UB40 card. At the Birmingham Locarno we played the first of two nights for under-eighteens only and Musical Youth supported us. Friars in Aylesbury was heavy. But I have fond memories of the

Coliseum in St Austell. It was one of the best nights of the tour and the audience was fantastic. They wanted to see us so much.

Before the tour we had advertised for bands to send in tapes if they wanted to support us. The band listened to the cassettes together and often I would take some home. If two or three of us liked a tape we would offer a band the opening slot. One of those acts was a three-piece outfit called The Mood Elevators who we had seen at the Barrel Organ, in Birmingham, the previous year. The band line-up was David Ditchfield, Noel Green, and Jenny Jones on vocals and drums, and their music was a bit weird and different so we liked that. We put a single out for them on Go Feet called 'Annapurna', which is a Himalayan mountain range, although The Mood Elevators used to tell people it was an Indian takeaway. Andy and Shuffle produced it billed as the Punjab Brothers. It wasn't a particularly commercial-sounding record and unsurprisingly it didn't chart. I produced the band's second single with Dave, a cover of The Seekers' hit 'Georgie Girl', for Red Records and added guest vocals on the B-side, 'You Never Try'.

The Go Feet deal with Arista allowed us to release six bands a year of our choice, and amongst the demo tapes we received we missed signing Wham! In George Michael's biography it says that they sent an 8-track demo to Go Feet when they were called The Executives. The tape included a song called 'Rude Boy', a cover of 'Can't Get Used To Losing You' and a ska version of Beethoven's 'Für Elise', no doubt influenced by Madness recording a nutty boys version of Tchaikovsky's 'Swan Lake'. John Mostyn turned Wham! down – without our knowledge, I hasten to add – but I can safely say, George and Andrew Ridgeley found their own image despite the knock-back.

We wanted to release more records on Go Feet but with touring and making our own records it took up too much time. More often than not we were exhausted from being on the road and we didn't have the energy to put into Go Feet. Sadly, beyond releasing Beat records, the label fizzled out.

Together with The Mood Elevators, the Au Pairs came on the *Wha'ppen?* tour, and then, from Manchester onwards, The Belle Stars took over. They were a seven-piece all-girl band that had formed after Rhoda Dakar and Nicky Summers had left The Bodysnatchers. By then, Rhoda was doing backing vocals with The Specials. She was a talented and intelligent woman who I've always been in awe of. We're all part of the 2 Tone posse. We got on with The Belle Stars. Neville [Staple] was going out with Stella Barker, their rhythm guitar player. She was good for him. Meantime, Dave had met a girl called Dominique, who was the cook and cleaner at Harrowby Court while we were recording, and they fell madly in love. Dave invited her to live with him in Birmingham and so I had to move on. We were on the road all the time and I was accumulating stuff and needed a place to keep it all, so I moved back home, took over my sister's room and set up a studio. It was great. I was getting wages and I could pay Mum rent.

After the British tour we did a short European tour taking in Germany, France and Holland. We chartered a private twin-engine plane to fly to Berlin and during the flight I asked to look in the cockpit. For a few seconds, they allowed me and Shuffle to take over the controls. The pilot would have lost his job if the authorities had found out but we were thrilled to have been given the brief opportunity to fly a plane. The final date in Amsterdam was a sell-out, but when we played 'Jackpot' about two dozen fans invaded the stage. Andy was nearly knocked off his feet, and Shuffle had to clamber to safety on a drum riser. Dave and I were surrounded by punks and skinheads with Alan, our bouncer, trying to protect us. After the gig, John Mostyn attempted to lift our spirits by opening a couple of bottles of champagne to celebrate the end of the tour, but it was difficult to raise our deflated mood.

During the British tour we witnessed a lot of deprivation and a growing dissatisfaction with Thatcherism and the ruling Conservative government. Since the introduction of the 'sus law' the police had been harassing a lot of black people. An 1824 Vagrancy Act was invoked, enabling the police to stop and search black youth for the smallest of suspicion. Police were always following you or slowing down in their panda cars when you were going about your business. Punks and Rastas never trusted the police, but Birmingham was different to London. We didn't all have a story about being arrested, and on marches the police, in general, appeared to be neutral. They were there to uphold the law and to protect, and to keep the National Front in order. That said, I was aware that there were a lot of racist policemen. You'd see it on the news every day. It was a fact of life in industrial cities where immigrants had come over in the Fifties and Sixties. There would be a racist attack and nothing would be done. Black youths were stopped far more than white youths; I was stopped and searched many times but I was smart enough not to get arrested by complying and being polite. My family are not violent. We use our heads, not our fists. Franco Rosso's film *Babylon* painted a realistic portrait of police harassment towards working-class black youth in late-Seventies Britain. It starred Brinsley Forde from Aswad, and also showed blues dances and the appeal of talking on the mic at sound systems. It was our world. The police raid in the final scene could have been wherever there was a black community.

The country was in deep economic decline and everywhere we went people were suffering, particularly the further north we travelled. There was an obvious north-south divide. Anger built up across Britain until inevitably people expressed their frustrations and rage by rioting on the streets of Handsworth, Bristol, London, Leeds, Manchester and Liverpool, forcing the government to listen. I called them the 'Prediction Riots' after the Steel Pulse song. They foresaw what was coming on *Handsworth Revolution*. During the rioting I drove to Handsworth and got close enough to see what was happening.

Police were everywhere and I could see people throwing objects and upturning cars. The whole area was out of control and I left quickly. The rioting spread and there were also minor disturbances in the city centre. I didn't have a grievance on the whole towards the police. It was important to have a police force to maintain law and order, otherwise there would be total anarchy. I didn't want to riot. I would have preferred to have marched, peacefully.

During the disturbances, we travelled to Manchester to record the first episode of a new children's Saturday morning show called *Get Set for Summer*, and spent the Friday evening watching blazing fires and SPG [Special Patrol Group] vans racing by from our hotel window. When we arrived at the studios we were welcomed by the spectacle of Buster Bloodvessel from Bad Manners teaching the 'Can Can' to the audience and one of the young presenters, Mark Curry. We had been booked to play three songs: 'Mirror In The Bathroom', 'Doors Of Your Heart' and 'Get-A-Job'. It was live. At the end of the third number we launched into an impromptu version of 'Stand Down Margaret' as a comment on the riots. All the band whipped off their jackets and displayed 'Stand Down Margaret' mushroom cloud T-shirts, accompanied by Buster Bloodvessel in a white dress and hastily thrown-on Beat T-shirt. I looked across to Peter Powell, the other presenter, and he was in shock. The BBC had given us free tickets for fan club members and much to our amusement the audience went crazy.

The same day, The Specials secured their second number one. 'Ghost Town' made total sense: no jobs meant angry people. It was a proper 'message to you' to the government. That's how Coventry and the UK was. The clubs had been closed down. There was nowhere to go. Nothing to do. Like The Beat, The Specials spoke about what was happening in society, and record-buyers vindicated the mood of the nation by sending that message to the top of the charts.

The following day we played the Lisdoonvarna Festival near Shannon in Ireland in front of 30,000 people. The only blazes were from campfires – a stark contrast to the troubles in England. We went on at 10.30 p.m. and Dave said to the audience, 'Thanks for building the fires… it makes us feel at home.' Saxa was on top form and added little improvised parts throughout the night. It was infectious. Before the encore I went out and did a spontaneous toast, and then, just as we played our last note, the heavens opened and we were treated to a spectacular Irish monsoon.

Unsurprisingly, in the wake of the summer riots and our political stance, there was growing negativity in the UK media towards the band. Fortunately, we were doing so well in America it didn't seem to matter, and we largely ignored it. I reasoned, 'You can't spend your life believing what the press say.' At the end of the day it's just one person's view. I judged a gig by the audience reaction. They were the people who had paid for a ticket regardless of what the critics had to say. The gigs were rocking, so we knew we were doing a good job. Nevertheless, our singles were underperforming.

Towards the end of the year the record company decided 'Hit It' was going to be our next single. It reached number seventy and spent only two weeks on the chart. It was the least successful Beat record issued. I was glad it wasn't a hit. It was one of the worst singles we put out. It sounded brash and harsh. Dave wrote the song about autoeroticism. I wasn't interested. It was one of a few Beat songs that I didn't like. The single was wrapped up in The Beat aiming for something different. We thought Bob Sargeant was playing it safe and getting soft. Arista had recently signed Haircut 100; Bob produced their first album, *Pelican West*. We didn't want their influence on our next record. They were mellower than us, although I got on with their singer, Nick Heyward – I've since been told he was a fan of 'Best Friend' and 'Mirror In The Bathroom'. However, our decision to go with a new producer who was a little more dangerous was, with hindsight, misguided.

Mike Hedges had produced and worked with artists like The Cure and Siouxsie & The Banshees. He drove a white Porsche with the number plate '3K' in honour of his favourite sound frequency; all the producers had their own frequency. With Mike lent 'Hit It' was an edgier, compressed production. But going with him was a mistake. It was the first time the band had played live in the studio since 'Tears Of A Clown' but the production didn't have any order. The Beat sound may have been chaotic but it was controlled. To add to our mounting dissatisfaction we gave *NME* an exclusive dub version of 'Hit It' for their *Dancin' Master* compilation series. And then, while we were in America, Arista sent them a version of the twelve-inch mix labelled as the single. *NME* said it sounded like 'a hazy, befuddled, jumble of half-conceived ideas, a seven-minute shadow of the real Beat'. Richard Cook went on to say that the 'distortion on the track was so severe that it had to be stopped mid-play', before rounding off his review with a dismissive 'not much cop'.

The disenchantment in the UK surrounding The Beat signposted a new beginning for the band. For us, it was like, 'Well, we've said everything we have to say politically,' so as the band got more popular in the States, we started writing more pop and love songs. The next batch of songs replaced political issues with personal politics: we live with politics and we live with people. There's politics in relationships. It was good to combine the two, and as they used to say in the Seventies, 'the personal is political'. It got us to the next level.

Around this time I started writing down my thoughts, which were published in our fanzine. It's been quite a surprise seeing them again for the first time in forty years but they give an interesting insight into the mind of my eighteen-year-old self coming to terms with the first flushes of success. There are seven short pieces.

I don't think there is any such
thing as a Pop Star?
You see, a group gets well-known
and then gets big headed about their hit
singles and albums.
Because they have been given so many
front pages in newspapers and magazines and because
they have had so such much radio and TV exposure
the people who buy their records see them as Idols.
That is what the telly makes you out to be.
We are no higher or lower than any of the people
who come to our gigs to see us.
I hate it when someone totally ignores you,
and as soon as you find out who you are
they're all over you.
The only kind of Star I know of is the
stars I see in the sky at night.
Thinking yourself as a Star is total vanity.
Most groups who think that way usually flop anyway.

What is a best friend?
Someone who walks around with you
everywhere you go.
Someone who sticks up for you.
Now imagine if I robbed a bank
and got ruffly around forty-million pounds.
Say I got caught but by then I had given

the money to you to look after till I came
out of prison seven years later.
Would you still be waiting to hand
me my money over?
Then I would know if you were
really my best friend or not.
But remember,
"A promise is a comfort to a fool."

Imagine if your mind could concentrate
on going further into the Universe than any
man could think.
Your house gets smaller as you penetrate into
the atmosphere, the World gets smaller and so
does the Moon and all the other planets around
it, past the sun, and past many other Universes.
And as you go through Eternity, you find that
All the Solar Systems and Universes eventually
seem to take the form of a man…
COULD THIS BE GOD?

If we are to believe in God,
why do Jehovah's Witnesses hate
the Catholics, why do Christians
Hate Rastas?
When you check it out nearly all
religions come to the same meaning.

So what religion should I defend?
If I go with one, another will
chant me down, and try to convert
me to theirs.
Man, what a confusion.

The amazing thing about Life
is that you just can't predict
what's going to happen next.

One thing that confuses me about the Bible is that,
"An eye for an eye and a tooth for a tooth."
Check the New Testament and Jesus says,
"Love your enemies."
If I was in a position where I was struck in the face,
which one would I take advice from?

How did this Universe come to be?
If God created the Universe,
then who created God?
God created himself, but how can
something create itself out of Nothing?
The Bible says that God was there from the beginning,
but I myself get really confused
when I think about these things.
Where did God come from? Heaven.
If Heaven is up in the skies, it must be

A long way for us to travel when we die.
Nobody knows where Heaven is,
for all we know it could be in the middle
of the Earth, or even right now
but in a different Time.

Life is like gambling in a way.
Like for instance playing chess,
whatever move you make is very important.
Like a school leaver today he or she has to decide
their next move,
whether to go to college or whether you go out
and look for a job in a country where
jobs are scarce, because that move controls your future.
To all people who say they never gamble,
"Remember, every single thing you do or
any word you say is a gamble."

I don't like frightening people, but let's just face a few
possibilities.......I think Ronald Reagan would just love
to start a war on Russia... but one thing people have to be
realise is that Europe is the first target – and that means US.
If the Reagan administration had their way, they would plant
their blood-shedding missiles in this country and they would
probably have total control over them... which means they
could start a war and we would take the blame for it – only
there wouldn't be a Britain to take the blame any more because

we would all be blown to bits before we knew what had happened. I heard old Ronnie on the news the other night, and I heard him talking about a limited nuclear war in Europe… if he thinks that way, then he can't have any feelings for people, although we are only human and our body systems work just like anyone else's… In the cowboy films, the American army always comes to the rescue at the last moment; this time I should pity myself if the cavalry came. This is why we need nuclear disarmament, or else we might as well call ourselves the Living Dead.

It's very serious, because the next one's the killer. If there is another one after that it would probably be in millions of years' time… I wonder what we would look like then? Cavemen or Gilagogs? …who knows? I only wrote all this because I had these funny thoughts in my mind, and I thought it would be good to let people know what I really think. We were put on this earth to live together, love and not kill Because Life is for Living.

The Limits We Set

Songwriting. *Special Beat Service*

Boredom was often a problem travelling, so when we went to America we introduced songwriting notepads on the tour bus. In the very early days, Dave was the main songwriter. Then I joined the band and added toasting to the songs. Naturally, the songwriting developed and Dave and I would pass each other suggestions. There was a lot of, 'Try this. Try that.' 'Oh, that sounds better.' By the time of the *Wha'ppen?* tour, somebody came up with the idea of everybody contributing ideas to lyrics. We each had a notepad – except Saxa, although he would often say things that would end up in lyrics – the idea being to write down anything which came into your mind, however rubbish it seemed, in case it could be useful to someone else. Then every couple of days we'd swap pads and carry on from where the last person had left off, or just simply write one-liners or couplets that came to mind. It gave you something to think about, and at the end of the tour all the notepads were collected and Andy and Dave went through them and picked out the best lines. Phrases from newspapers were often combined, and the lyrics for 'Cheated' and 'Dream Home In NZ' were taken from an assortment of current affairs reports. Andy, in particular, liked trivia. He liked to get into different ways of making things and understanding how they worked. I may not have understood the meaning to all the songs but I got the gist. The pressure of writing hit songs didn't come until later, when Dave and I had formed General Public. The Beat smelt of hit songs. It was just the style of music we made. Whatever we played just needed an added hook line. The music carried it through. It wasn't so much the pressure of writing hits that we felt, but making sure we didn't sell out by becoming too commercial. That was always my thing. The underground side of The Beat was its longevity and the more overtly commercial songs were for the immediate. 'Twist And Crawl' (number nine), 'Mirror In The Bathroom' (number four), and 'Too Nice To Talk To' (number seven) was the dark side of The Beat. 'Tears Of A Clown' (number six) and 'Can't Get Used To Losing You' (number three) was the light side.

By the release of our third album, *Special Beat Service*, we were all writing bits and pieces and all being equally credited, dividing the publishing six ways, whether one person predominantly wrote a tune or not. The Beat was a democracy.

It reflected the principle behind the band. We all had an equal voice. If any one of us had something to say it would be listened to.

Special Beat Service was a play on words taken from the Special Boat Service, which had been established by the Royal Navy for covert operations in World War Two. It was also the name of the first unit to be dispatched to the Falkland Islands during the conflict in 1982, and I have a memory of us all listening to a debate in the House of Commons about the war while we were recording the album. For Margaret Thatcher, the conflict would help to propel her and the Conservatives to a second landslide general election victory the following year. For The Beat, the new album was an opportunity to cross over to a mainstream audience and potentially conquer the American market.

Initially, we didn't know which way to go stylistically with the third album, but as we began to record the sound started to lean towards African influences. You can hear it on 'She's Going'. If some songs were veering towards a world music sound, 'Save It For Later' was more attributable to the rhythmic drone of The Velvet Underground. Dave wrote *save it for later* as a play on *save it, fellator*. The song dated back to Dave and Andy's time in the Isle of Wright. They used to play it at the Mercat Cross and it was one of the songs that made me want to be in The Beat in the first place. 'Save It For Later' sounded like a hit, but in the nascent days of the band, Shuffle said it was 'too rock... too old wave' so it got dropped. It was a classic as far as I was concerned. The accompanying video was made by Julien Temple and offered a different interpretation from the sexual side of the lyrics. The storyline centred on the band playing in an underground cavern dressed in Sixties-style outfits to match the feel of the song. The audience are seen reading books like *Animal Farm* and *Das Kapital* but by the middle of the song they're all on their feet dancing. The girl I danced with was really beautiful, but unfortunately I never saw her again.

'Save It For Later' was the lead single from *Special Beat Service* and one of the best songs we ever recorded. I loved the atmosphere created by the jangling guitars. It was a cousin to 'Best Friend' – they share the same key and tuning – but surprisingly it didn't chart very highly in the UK, only reaching number forty-seven. The *NME* wrote that the band had lost its 'former zing and zeal'. By contrast, 'Save It For Later' did really well in America, featuring on many film soundtracks. Pete Townshend used to play it at his solo concerts and recorded a version of the song during the sessions for his *White City* album. And in the Nineties, Pearl Jam included 'Save It For Later' in their live set. It was a wonderful compliment and I'm thrilled that the song has continued to have a life beyond The Beat.

During the sessions for *Special Beat Service* we recorded an advert for Freddie Laker's 'no frills' airline, over the backing track of 'The Limits We Set'. Laker Airways had the cheapest flights in the world and in our eyes, it was the people's airline because it was affordable. We used to fly Laker to New York from the UK and internally within the States. We thought if we recorded a jingle for the company we might get free flights for life. We sent the recording to the airline company but the business was made bankrupt in 1982 and the jingle went down with it. Another unreleased track was 'It Makes Me Rock', which struggled to find a place on the album. We tried it in many different ways but it never really worked. It was eventually released on a deluxe edition of *Special Beat Service* twenty years later. A third unreleased recording was a version of a Cole Porter song from the musical *Gay Divorce*. Both Fred Astaire and Frank Sinatra had previously recorded 'Night And Day', and we tested out our version on a Radio 1 session for the Kid Jensen Show almost as a laugh to be the opposite of what people might expect of The Beat.

It wasn't untypical for songs to come along and then get dropped. In the early days we had a tune called 'Motor Show' – *we're all going to the Motor Show*. It was about capitalism and more obviously the British International Motor Show, which used to be held in Birmingham at the National Exhibition Centre. I used to say, 'That's a hit.' It had a 'Twist And Crawl' style bass line. It was a great tune and we used to play it live but unfortunately never recorded it.

'Spar Wid Me' was a track that I wrote for the third album. If someone is your 'spa' they are your friend and you move around together. It was the opposite of 'spar' meaning 'to fight'. The song centred on the 'one-drop', which naturally made it sound closer to UB40's style and sound. 'Spar Wid Me' came out of a jam session. Shuffle said, 'Here's one for you, a simple one,' and played the bass line. Although, I seem to remember we did a new John Peel Session around this time, before the album recording, where the bass line was totally different. Another song I played a key part in came as a result of listening to 'Mirror In The Bathroom'. Somehow the tape messed up and played the track backwards. I said to Dave, 'Listen to this. We could take the bass line and use it for a new song.' Shuffle worked out the bass line in reverse and it became 'Rotating Heads'.

'Jeanette' was named after a girl Dave used to go out with who had a beehive hairdo and who worked at the dole office when we were signing on. Although, I've heard Dave claim it's more of an archetype about a rich girl who likes to hang out with musicians. Either way, the accordions lent 'Jeanette' a joyful French feel, even though it was a sad song. And the play on words and internal rhymes were very clever.

> *When I met Jeanette*
> *Substitute Ronette*
> *She said, will you remember*
> *I said, I could never forget her*
> *Au naturalette*

Her mom's a millionette
So we shared one last cigarette and swapped false addresses

Sadly, like its predecessor, 'Save It For Later', 'Jeanette' barely scraped into the Top 50, peaking at number forty-five and only staying on the singles chart for three weeks, but at least every time we put a single out we sold another ten or twenty thousand albums that week.

I like to claim that I discovered Pato Banton and gave him his first break in the music business. Pato won a toasting competition that I judged at the Imperial Cinema on the Moseley Road in Balsall Heath. The prize was £50, which was a lot of money back then. Pato was obviously the best toaster on the day, but I also thought he was far superior and more advanced than I was. He had the crowd in his power. He told funny stories about his family and did impressions of his mum. I said to him after, 'Me and you will have to do something together.' He was well up for it. The next time I saw the band, I said, 'I've found this MC. I want to do something with him. He's a really nice guy.' The resulting 'Pato And Roger Ago Talk' was a jam we originally recorded around the same time as 'Hit It'. 'Ago' means 'going to'. General Saint & Clint Eastwood had just released 'Tribute To General Echo', which combined their toasting, so the timing was really good for MC duos. We cut 'Pato And Roger Ago Talk' as a solo record and issued it as a double A-side with 'Cool Entertainer', credited to Ranking Roger as opposed to The Beat. I did an MC over the band's backing track of 'Which Side Of The Bed?' The verses were freestyle and when I ran out of ideas I went back to the chorus:

I don't need no Trainer
A little influence of pen and little paper
That's what you need to be a cool entertainer

The band talked me into having 'Pato And Roger Ago Talk' on *Special Beat Service* and we used a version I mixed with Mike Hedges.

It was at this time that we had to retire Saxa. He said his health was failing and he was getting too old to be on the road. Saxa was often ill and he always told us he was dying. He was given a health warning by a GP and had to give up his breakfast diet of brandy and eggs. He then discovered Budweiser, renamed it 'Dubweiser', and lived on for another forty years. As a replacement, Dave brought in Wesley Magoogan on saxophone after seeing him in the film *Breaking Glass* with Hazel O'Connor. Wesley had a harsher sound which I didn't like for The Beat. It was never the same without Saxa. Sadly, after The Beat split up, Wesley had an accident with a circular saw and lost the use of his fingers.

Overall, *Special Beat Service* could have been better. It was kind of like a combination of the first two records. Bob did a good job with what we offered him and made it accessible to radio, but when I listen to it now I hear the mistakes. In 'Sole Salvation' for instance, some of the drum rolls were out of time. I didn't like every song. And unbeknown to any of us at the time, *Special Beat Service* would be the last Beat album.

Part Four:
America, Roger and Out

An Organised Revolution

The Clash. US festival. Rasta

When I first heard The Clash I didn't like them. I thought, 'This music is too brash, man.' I was more into the Sex Pistols. They were the main punk band. For a band who claimed that they couldn't play their instruments, *Never Mind The Bollocks* sounded bloody good. It was so musical and well produced but also raw. I also liked *The Great Rock 'n' Roll Swindle*, which had a more polished sound. The Clash were not polished until *Sandinista!* I really got into them around *London Calling* when I saw them live. 'Ah, I get it now.' Records and playing live are two different things. People expect you to sound like your records. Thank God bands don't. The Clash were a better live band than they were on record. The atmosphere at their gigs was thrilling and they were more experimental, with extended jams and dubs. You'd hear mistakes but that was where the magic came from. After I'd heard all those tunes live, I went back to the first and second albums, and I could take songs like 'I'm So Bored With The USA', and 'White Riot'. And I'd always loved '(White Man) In Hammersmith Palais'.

By the time I knew The Clash, the punk scene had died and they were pop stars. They had a security guard called Raymond, who had dreadlocks and was from St Kitts. He would always take me backstage to see Mick and Joe. They knew The Beat and kept on saying, 'One day you should come and play with us.' Then in September 1981 they booked an eight-night stand at Théâtre Mogador in Paris and invited us to open for them. They were some of the best gigs The Beat ever did. We got on like a house on fire. The Clash were like brothers-in-arms. They were cool guys and didn't behave like rock stars at all. I befriended Mick and we would smoke weed together. Joe was a man you had to pick the right time to deal with. He had a lot going on in his mind, but he was all right with me. I was only seventeen and Joe was ten years older than me. He saw me as one of the young ones coming through. I also got on really well with Paul Simonon. He was the reggae man. He had all the original Jamaican seven-inch records with no middle in them – a sign of a serious collector. Paul had learnt to play by listening to Studio One records. You could hear it in his bass lines, like 'Guns Of Brixton' and 'Bankrobber'.

At the first Paris date, I was standing on Paul's side of the stage when Joe looked over to me and said, 'Come on.'

Then he turned back to the audience, and started saying, 'R-R-Roger', rolling the 'R', and the audience started clapping on the beat. The Clash were playing 'Armagideon Time' so I took a mic and toasted the first thing that came into my head: *Nice up the dance, nice up the dance.* Then they went into 'Police And Thieves' and I started saying *sky lily, sky lily, lily, lily, lily, lily* – it didn't mean anything. It was just a melody that sounded good to get the audience on my side. I used to pick up on sounds like that, or if I hit upon a hook line I'd use it. When one of your heroes comes up to you and says, 'Right, we want you on stage, now,' you say, 'Okay!' You don't think about it. All I knew was that they wanted me to MC and do something different, not just *police and thieves*, and I wanted to keep the audience going. Compared to The Beat, it was different toasting to a Clash audience. Their audience was rougher because The Clash had been a punk band. If you were crap, a punk audience would throw bottles or spit at you, and you could still sense that edge of potential hostility.

I was outside the dressing room the next day and I heard them talking: 'We don't want no other fucker in here. Roger comes on stage with us so he's one of us. He's all right.' I was like, 'Bloody hell. That's like family, man.' I went in and Joe gave me this specially designed T-shirt with the arms cut off, which they all wore. He said, 'Here you are. Wear this on stage tonight.' That night I toasted on 'Armagideon Time' and Mikey Dread did a version of 'Bankrobber', which he produced as a single for The Clash, coupled with the B-side 'Rockers

Galore', aptly labelled 'Dread at the Controls'. Mikey was a quiet man. He had released an album called *African Anthem* in 1978, on which he mixed echo, sound effects and people talking together. For The Clash, it was an authentic link to reggae. Mikey and I talked about doing something together but it never happened. Pearl Harbour also joined us at some point during the set. Pearl was dangerous. If you messed with her she could open her mouth and hold her own. She was fit and gorgeous. After the show, I said, 'Thank you, Joe,' and handed back the T-shirt. He said, 'No. You keep that. That's yours. You're one of us, now.' That was something to behold.

After Paris, The Clash invited us to support them in America: first in Hollywood and then two nights in San Francisco. They then asked us to go to Canada with them but we couldn't afford it. The short tour started off as two nights at the Hollywood Palladium, which held almost four thousand people. It was sold out. We were added to the bill and it turned into five sold-out shows. They were the wildest audiences I'd ever seen. Beat and Clash mania broke out over Hollywood; everybody wanted to see the show and we became the talk of the town. They couldn't get enough of the two bands. Bob Dylan came to one of the shows but we never met him. I have great memories of that tour. One night, The Clash wanted Mikey Dread and me to have a live toasting competition on stage and Paul was winking conspiratorially to the others. We were saying, 'No. We don't want to compete with each other.' But following our set I would go on stage with them most nights to MC on 'Police And Thieves' or 'Armagideon Time'. We got a little thing going. They were some of the best gigs we ever did. In fact, if I had to single out the best moment in all my time with The Beat, it would be that run of shows. It was a magical experience. We had the most amazing energy on stage and played our hearts out. The tour melded both bands and we became proper buddies. I got to know them intimately. I was always in their dressing room. There was great banter and we'd all go to clubs together after the gigs.

We did a couple of tours with The Clash. Both bands complemented and liked each other. We were about the same things: equality, individuality, fairness. The Clash had more anger than The Beat and an element of punk rebel destruction. Some nights I could hear them arguing on stage: 'Fuck off,' 'You fuck off.' When it was bad it was bad. Mick would have a go at Joe, or vice versa, and then Mick would have a go at the roadies. Then other nights everything would be perfect. Like most bands, they had interpersonal problems, but once they were on stage they created this fantastic sound and vibe. You had to be there to capture their essence. It was never the same watching them on film or listening to a live recording. As soon as they ran on the stage, the barrier between them and the audience would come down. They would be dressed in militant clothes, looking all swanky and meaning business. Joe, Mick and Paul would stand in a line at the front of the stage and then the camouflage curtain would rise and they would be off. The whole thing was like an organised revolution and the crowd just took to it. Every night the vibe was different. It was the same with The Beat. Every gig was brilliant. It was amazing to be part of it. And the way Strummer sang. He would do his wailing and that was it. He was a true leader. The Clash were anthem-bringers.

In between dates with The Clash we continued to tour in the States, and I have fond memories of two sold-out nights in New York's downtown, but fashionable, Ritz. It had been a year since we had last played there. One fan, Bud Kliment, sent a review to *The Noise In This World* which neatly describes the show: 'Opening with "Twist And Crawl" and proceeding through a set drawn largely from *I Just Can't Stop It* and *Wha'ppen?*, The Beat were very tight, rocking and seemed to be enjoying themselves immensely. Roger was resplendent in black from head to toe, wearing a touch of red, green and gold; Andy had on a Hawaiian shirt, Shuffle opted for a paisley one; Everett, on the other hand, was bare-chested; Dave was dapper in white shirt and dark vest, and Saxa – this was before he had retired – wore brightly patched pants and shirt and a grin that was at least a mile wide. In total, the band did nearly twenty songs, including a surprise "Psychedelic Rockers" (which never actually got released in this country) and the official, off the record debut of "Hit It". They also did a surprisingly good "Walk Away" and later tidily alternated the words "Stand Down Ronald" with "Stand Down Margaret". The Ritz audience was always attentive and enthusiastic, most especially so for the fastest dance numbers like "Mirror In The Bathroom", "Click Click" and "Ranking Full Stop". The band got two encores, which in New York City is pretty rare... The Beat not only made it here, they tore the roof off the sucker.'

On Labor Day weekend, September 1982, we played the US Festival in the Glen Helen Regional Park, San Bernardino. It was organised by Steve Wozniak, who co-founded Apple Computers. He used his money to put on his favourite musicians instead of handing it over to the taxman. It was a massive tax giveaway. The park had the biggest stage in the world, the biggest PA, the biggest lights, the biggest audience. All the acts arrived by helicopter – The Police, Talking Heads, The B-52's, The Kinks, Tom Petty & The Heartbreakers, Fleetwood Mac, The Ramones, Pat Benatar – all day you saw choppers taking off and coming in, flying in the stars.

We played on the opening night with Talking Heads and The Police, and as we descended over the site we saw an incredible mass of people. It was amazing. People as far as you could see. Four days earlier, we had supported The Police at the Gateshead International Stadium when U2 were also on the bill; U2 opened for us three months later at the Hammersmith Palais and nearly blew us off stage. They were brilliant and the crowd was electric – I had a pair of trousers made for the gig with a red, gold and green stripe down the leg, and during 'Too Nice To Talk To' I played Roto-toms – a small shell-less drum tuneable by rotation. They were only a couple of inches thick but sounded really powerful. The gig was a big deal and we went down a storm. It was the first time we had played in front of such a huge audience in England, but nothing could have prepared us for the size of the audience in the San Bernardino desert.

Before we went on stage, The Beat had a special handshake. We would lock hands and then Dave and I used to look into each other's eyes, and say, 'Lion'. It was to give each other confidence to go out and perform. 'We're in this together, man.' When I walked out at the US Festival I was confronted with was a sea of faces as far as the eye could see. I was like, 'My God! Where do you start here?' We were so nervous. That was the biggest gig we ever did. It was the biggest gig any musician had ever done. Playing in front of half a million people. It was like, 'How are they going to hear us in time at the back?' They had PA stacks going all the way back and they were all slightly delayed and synchronised, but I'm sure from that distance away it would have looked like I was dancing out of time.

The Beat were the only band to play the US Festival two years running. It was a testament to our music. The following year, four nights were staged over Memorial Day Weekend and each night was dedicated to a different genre. We were invited to play on New Wave Day with INXS, A Flock Of Seagulls, Stray Cats, Men At Work and The Clash and got paid £250,000. On Rock Day, David Bowie got £2.2 million. We were used to getting ten or fifteen grand a gig and here was this guy offering us £¼ million for an hour's set. Why would we argue with that? If we'd argued for £½ million they probably would have given it to us but we weren't like that. If you're too greedy you miss the whole point. We opened with 'Mirror In The Bathroom' and the cheer from the crowd was deafening. It's reported the attendance was 670,000. From the stage, the audience looked like a million birds flapping their wings. When I introduced 'Ranking Full Stop' I said, 'Are you ready? Said are you ready to dance?' The crowd went mad and I launched into a freestyle toast: *Here comes the musical thing keep you rocking and swing so all you got to do is keep on coming down and don't be no bore or no whore as I will you tell about the sound that you keep you rocking and sway all the way down there.* Everett cracked the snare roll, Shuffle ran across the stage and the bass and the drums were totally out of time with each other. It took a couple of bars for it to drop in and link. The Beat was always hit and miss like that. You never knew when there was going to be a duff drum roll. Everett played so fast sometimes you couldn't keep up with him. I'd listen back to gig recordings and they were twice as fast as the records. I'd be like, 'What are you guys on, man?' But then everyone would catch up with each other. Those moments were really good. If Everett was on form we would groove all night. To this day, people still talk about The Beat at the US Festivals. But the next thing I knew The Clash had kicked Mick Jones out of the band so the festival turned out to be the last gig he played with them. I couldn't believe it because they were sounding so good.

While we had been on tour with The Clash the previous year, Joe and Mick kept on saying, 'When we're back in London come and do something with us. Drop some lines on "Rock The Casbah" and we can put out a twelve-inch version of it.' I went down to Sonic Studios in Notting Hill and met Mick and a couple of engineers. Joe wasn't around. I went into the live room, put the cans on and they played the backing track. It was the original 24-track and they just took Joe's lead vocal out. I had a run through and then I stopped, and said, 'Start taking.' Mick said, 'We took what you were doing – let's do another!' I had a hook line from doing it on tour – *come on everybody, mek we do the Casbah, Rock the Casbah* – so I did another two tracks of freestyle. It didn't really matter what else I said because as I say, all people want to hear is the chorus. They don't listen to the verses. What I laid down was an MC version to complement their song:

> *I said a special request to the Clash drummer*
> *and special request to Joe Strummer.*

It rhymed!
Another line was:

> *Paul Simonon on the bass just off low*
> *and the one Mick Jones with Should I Stay or Should I Go?*

There was humour in it. It was a guide vocal so I could get more ideas, but Mick was happy, and said, 'We've got it.' I also did a toast over 'Red Angel Dragnet' – *they shoot the wrong man and they ruin the plan.* It was about the film editor, Stephen Waldorf, who was shot by the Metropolitan Police, who in turn claimed they had mistaken Waldorf for the fugitive David Martin. I also did some lines about the nuclear threat:

> *di Russian di American dem both have a plan*
> *and if we no careful they involve a England*
> *So what's the worry? It's the cruise missile*
> *cause if we not careful we end up in a pile.*

The engineer gave me a rough mix of the tracks to take home. I made a copy and gave the original tape to John Peel. I said, 'I have this. You're not allowed to play it (wink, wink).' Of course, Peel played it on his Radio 1 show. I was like, 'Great!'

Sadly, neither version of 'Rock The Casbah' or 'Red Angel Dragnet' was ever officially released. In time, both mixes made their way onto a bootleg album, but it wasn't very good quality. It sounded like both tracks had been recorded off the radio.

After the US Festival in May 1983, The Clash soldiered on without Mick Jones, but it was the never the same. The next time I saw him was in the Nineties when I ended up joining Mick's band Big Audio Dynamite. We wrote some lyrics together called 'Moseley Girls'. I was living on Greenhill Road in Moseley at the time and he came to visit me. I took him into the village and we were bumping into fans and various people. Mick loved the vibe and kept on going on about Moseley girls. We got back to my place, got a pad out, and started writing down words between us, grabbing the pen whenever one of us had an idea. The song has never been recorded. In fact, the words still need a melody, so the joy of seeing Mick Jones/ Ranking Roger on a song credit will have to wait.

If you watch footage of The Beat at the first US Festival you will see I had dreadlocks, and by the second one, a year later, I had had them cut off. We were playing a sold-out show in New York, and I went into a famous Italian barbers and said, 'OFF.' The hairdresser couldn't believe it, and said, 'No. I can't.' I said, 'Skinhead. Everything off.' As I left, I went to put my hat back on and it didn't fit properly. I looked like Freddie 'Parrot-face' Davies. I had to put rolled-up paper around the brim of the hat to make it stay in place. I went back to the venue but I didn't tell or show the others what I'd done. Usually, on stage, after the third number I would take my hat off, shake my locks, and the crowd would cheer. We finished 'I Confess' and I flung my hat into the audience. There was an almighty gasp, and I shouted, 'RASTA BALDHEAD!'

I first grew dreads when I was about seventeen. A musician could get away with having locks but if you were a man on the street you would never get a job. Initially, you don't comb your hair and you have to part and shape the locks so that they don't form into large binds. At first it was difficult and I let a few binds grow in the wrong way. It was cool to have them because they weren't easy to grow, but I wasn't a Rastafarian. I was a fashion dread. Then after cutting my locks off in the

States I grew them again during Special Beat and I have had them ever since.

Rasta is not a religion, for me. It's a way of life: to be at one with the earth; to be organic; to avoid preservatives. People are now paying attention to that way of being. I was brought up a Catholic, and in many ways, it's a contradiction because Rastafarians see Rome as Babylon, which dates back to the Italian invasion of Ethiopia in 1935. My Catholic upbringing was the cause of a lot of confusion. I didn't have a physical being as a mentor. As kids, we taught each other and listened to records: by Big Youth and Peter Tosh and Lee Scratch Perry. They had a profound effect on the way I turned out. Some people would quote their Bibles but I put *Haile Selassie is God* to one side and started to read and study. The majority of black people I knew were Jamaican and the influence of 'Babylon must fall' and black oppression caught on. When I joined The Beat, Rastas would say, 'You're living in Babylon. Be careful of the white guys.' They didn't realise it was the white guys who were looking after my arse. People say you have to go with your gut feeling. I wholeheartedly agree with that. I knew being in The Beat was the right thing for me to do. Once we started having hits I became cool amongst the Rastas. They saw me as the first British MC to get into the charts. 2 Tone wasn't necessarily for Rastas but Beat music they could relate to because of the message of love and unity. We didn't sing about Jah, but we sang about people.

Linton Kwesi Johnson was one of the first black artists who made that artistic and spiritual connection by forging a link with Rock Against Racism. As well as supporting The Beat, he played gigs with PiL and Siouxsie & The Banshees, and successfully reached a white audience with a black conscience. Linton was a non-compromising poet, who you thought might be a Black Panther, writing words about abuse and how black people were being treated. I sympathised with the way he wrote. *Forces Of Victory* was a powerful album and 'Sonny's Lettah' could make a grown man cry. It was cleverly done.

Beyond music, my Rasta beliefs extended to possessions. One of the first moments of realisation came as result of a photo shoot we did for *Smash Hits*. It was a fun magazine to do. They used the backlight as a mock umbrella and I held it over Dave's head to make him look like a saint with a halo. When I saw the pictures in the magazine they looked great but I didn't like the fact I was brandishing jewellery. I had a silver ring and a couple of gold ones. I took them off and threw the vanity away. It was the Rasta head saying, 'Money is the root of all evil.' To me, food, air and life are the three important things in my life.

The Bad Angel

REM. Beat split

REM were one my favourite bands that opened up for The Beat. I loved Peter Buck's guitar style. Every night, half of The Beat would watch them play from the side of the stage. If you're the support band and the main act is watching you, you're doing good, but they didn't think that they were good. They were shy guys. Michael Stipe was always very nervous and you would find him in a sweat before going on. I remember saying to him before one show, 'Go out there and just do it because one day you guys are going to be massive.' He didn't believe me. He'd say, 'What! Us?' I could see the potential in REM – I saw the same in The Go-Go's and The Bangles early on – but it took a while for them to find their audience. When they supported us at Rissmillers, Reseda, in Los Angeles, a reviewer wrote:

'Following the upbeat Untouchables, REM came on and played some weird slow psychedelic music. The boos started by the second song, when the crowd realised it wasn't just an opener, it was the act itself, and Michael Stipe was onstage acting rather gay. At first it was boos, but then in the third song it started with cups of beer and then various small objects were thrown at Stipe on the stage, with some striking him square on the cheek. Ouch! REM quickly left the stage, and shortly thereafter The English Beat came on and restored dance music to the hall.'

As I remember, REM finished their set, otherwise I would have said something to the audience. I got on really well with Michael and Peter and I would have defended REM from beginning to end. When they became one of biggest pop bands in the world I was delighted.

I should explain that in the States we were known as The English Beat, as it says in the review. This was simply due to contractual reasons, because Paul Collins had a band called The Beat in Los Angeles who formed before we did in the UK. Rather than face a lawsuit from his record company we added the prefix 'English', and when in the UK they became Paul Collins' Beat.

By the time of *Special Beat Service* we were so big in America. We were playing to twenty thousand people a night. Not getting any time off. It was gig after gig after gig. We still hadn't had a hit and it seemed like everybody was saying to us, 'How come you're selling out these enormous venues and you're not in the Top 10?' We were doing bigger and bigger gigs and Dave and I were doing all the radio, TV and media interviews.

Even though, within the band, we saw each other as equals, people saw Dave and I as the face of The Beat. That got to my head, and believing that created a split within the band.

All my favourite bands split up after arguing – The Clash, The Specials, The Selecter. In the beginning everyone was thrown into a whirlwind of rock 'n' roll; some were stitched up contractually, some weren't. In The Beat, we thought it was best to talk about everything in the open. We didn't argue. We had sense. It was only near the very end where success went to our heads. Dave and I would talk very openly with each other. He would say, 'Roge, if you and I leave The Beat and form our own band we could go fifty-fifty instead of one sixth each. Think about that?' I was like, 'No man. This is the thing that we've got. You can't break it up. It's a living entity and it's getting bigger. We're bigger than we've ever been.' A few days later, he would try again: 'You've got some great tunes, Roger. Think about the publishing. You won't be getting one sixth any more you'll be getting 100 per cent because you wrote the song.' I wasn't interested, but I would say, 'Oh yeah? It sounds good. I'll think about it.' Then the next time, Dave would say, 'Who are the fans asking for? It's me and you, Roger.' Dave was like the bad angel on your left shoulder while the good angel was saying, 'No, Roger. You need to keep this together. Look how far you've got. Look where you're going. Are you going to start a new band like Terry, Neville and Lynval [Fun Boy Three] or because Mick Jones has started Big Audio Dynamite?' But that got me thinking, 'It's the new fashion to break up and start afresh.' I always dared to be different so I began to consider the idea of forming a new band. The seed was planted.

To be frank, on tour, The Beat members were quite boring so I started to travel with the road crew because they were more exciting. The others would say, 'The luxury is on the band bus. You're missing out, man.' I felt more at home with the crew. I recall on one tour we were coming out of Toronto where they were very relaxed about smoking weed. Usually, I was always very careful when we crossed a border, but on this occasion, unbeknown to me a couple of spliffs had fallen into my bag. We came to the crossing at the Peace Bridge and the US security stopped the van and searched it. The driver was saying, 'If they find anything they'll confiscate the vehicle and charge us for possession.' Inevitably, the joints were found in my bag and I had to put my hand up and admit they were mine. And then to everyone's surprise all I was given was an on-the-spot fine. We got to the gig and told the stage crew what had happened. It turned out that four hours earlier they had come through the checkpoint with both weed and cocaine and they also were just given fine. It was fortunate the incidents happened at Peace Bridge, which was renowned for its leniency, and we laughed it off.

The punk rebel side of me was still there and I saw the crew as mischievous. They were always playing up, whereas The Beat were all golden boys, in their own ways: listening to music; or watching a movie, but not horror or films with violence. But you could with the road crew. I used to carry equipment and the crew were forever pleading with me, 'Roger, please don't help us. You're a big star now.' I was like, 'What do you mean "big star"? You've made it worse now. I'm definitely coming with you tomorrow and humping the gear.' It wasn't until we were overworked and we began to fly everywhere that I had to stop helping.

One of the last gigs The Beat did in America was in front of 10,000 people at Red Rocks in Denver, Colorado. REM and Bow Wow Wow supported. *Special Beat Service* was on the Billboard Top 40 but we hadn't had a hit single and everyone, from our fans to the promoters, was saying, 'What's going on?' It was the same in California: we played massive theatres and convention centres in Los Angeles, San Francisco and San Diego, and sold them all out. I couldn't understand it. On the one hand we were selling out gigs and on the other our records sales were disappointing. The problem was our record company. We were on a small label and it could only get us so far. *I Just Can't Stop It* was licensed to Sire Records and then we moved to IRS, which was owned by Miles Copeland, the brother of Stewart. It was a subsidiary of A&M and more like an indie label. *Special Beat Service* reached number thirty-seven on the Billboard chart. 'Save It For Later' got to number fifty-eight and 'I Confess' number thirty-four. It created a buzz, but the campaign was lacking. Maybe IRS didn't want to put any more money into the band. We needed plugging and an extra push. Perhaps a fourth album would have taken us all the way, but all that time spent touring in America went to our heads.

(Above) with Murphy, 1983 © *Pennie Smith*; (right) me, Murphy and Angela.

(Opposite, above) General Public
rehearsing at Rockfield Studios;
(below) me, Angela and Mick
Jones.

(Above) General Public at the
Crompton Arms with Mick Jones
on guitar, December 1983.

(Left) with Madonna at *The Saturday Show*, March 3, 1984 © *ITV/Shutterstock*; (above) Mickey Billingham, Kevin White, me, Dave Wakeling, Horace Panter, Stoker, 1984. © *Joel Selvin/Getty*; (right) General Public, circa 1984.

(Above) with Pato Banton, 'Bubbling Hot' video shoot, 1994 © Mark Allan; (right) Special Beat, me and Neville Staples, circa 1992.

(Opposite, above) Robbie Shakespeare, me and Sly Dunbar, circa 1985 © Bob Berger; (opposite, below) The Selecter onstage at the Roundhouse with Pauline Black (centre) and Arthur 'Gaps' Hendrickson (right) © Lorne Thomson/Getty

(Above) performing
with Murphy at the
Roundhouse, October
6, 2017 © *Lorne
Thomson/Redferns/
Getty Images*

We were playing with some super big groups and we nabbed a lot of their fans who saw us as demigods. Before a show, I always used to walk around the auditorium to soak up the vibe and to get a feel for how to deal with the audience once I got on stage. It's a custom of mine. By that time it was impossible. As soon as I stepped out there'd be fifty people wanting a piece of me. I never got any peace and quiet. It was stressful for all of us. Acclaim changes you. When people continually tell you how important you are you can't but believe it. That makes a man act differently. I would say to people, 'Why am I so important?' They would say, 'You're in The English Beat, man! You're big! You're a star! You tour with The Clash! Your next album's going to go Top 10!' I'd say, 'What significance is that to the universe?' I didn't want to have to deal with pop star shit but everywhere we went there were red carpets and private chartered flights and five star hotels. I like to think I tried to keep my feet on the ground but I know I lost it for a while. I found I didn't care as much and I was bored with people. It affected us all in different ways. Dave and I were the targets. People would flock to us. Andy and Shuffle didn't like the limelight and used to run away from everyone. Everett wasn't really bothered. I was a bit diva-ish and came back to my senses too late. My friends in Birmingham had always told me if I changed they'd duff me up. I thought, 'I can't go back to England being like this.' But as they say, 'When in Rome'. I was trying to be an Englishman in America.

I used to share a room with Dave, so I understood where he was coming from. That's why it became Roger and Dave in the end. We'd toured too much with The Police; Dave thought he was Sting. He wanted to sound like him, dress like him, be like him. I used to think, 'Just be yourself. That's what you are.' You can see it in the performance of 'Too Nice To Talk To' on *Top of the Pops*. The rest of us were all looking at each other, as if to say, 'What's he thinking!'

The band was on one level and Dave was thinking on another. Still, we were good buddies and we only ever had a couple of near fights. One of them was while we were touring the first album. We had twelve dates booked in Europe during the early summer. It was our first trip abroad and we had a new tour manager, a certain Mr Norton, who was a shady character. We were driving through Europe, Norway I think, and we were all tired and we had a long drive ahead. Suddenly, a lorry appeared out of nowhere and tried to overtake a truck on our side of the road. It was a single narrow carriageway and the oncoming vehicle was speeding head on towards our bus. Our driver swerved and we skidded across the gravel verge as the other two vehicles sped past side-by-side. Miraculously, nobody was hurt and nothing was damaged. That could have been the end of The Beat. It was certainly a close shave. We drove on but tension rose between me and Dave as the realisation hit us that we could have all lost our lives. And then we went for each other. Perhaps it was the effects of shock. It was a just a matter of seconds and then the others pulled us back: 'No! Not here.

None of that.' I then had a sudden moment of realisation. I was saying to myself, 'Remember where you are. You're with The Beat.' We were a diplomatic band. We didn't fight each other. We reasoned with each other. That was the beauty of The Beat. That was what first appealed to me about the band and stopped me wanting to join UB40 or any another band. The Beat was about fighting through words; words of encouragement. If you had something negative to say you backed it up with something positive and with encouragement. That was always the strategy to deal with Beat members. It's amazing we were all like that. I've never known a band like it. Since then, I've thought about that incident with Dave hundreds of time and concluded it was because of tension and that we nearly died.

By late spring 1984, we had finished touring in America. We came back to England and spent three weeks in a rehearsal space jamming and getting new ideas together. The plan was to record a fourth Beat album. I've got tapes of the rehearsals filled with great ideas. The atmosphere and mood amongst us all was good. It didn't feel like the band was going to split up. But talk of forming a new band with Dave continued. The problem was Dave changed his mind every five minutes. He started getting the name 'difficult Dave' for his diva behaviour. If you watch the video for 'I Confess', you'll know what I mean. Dave was very insecure and everything was hot cold hot cold. It annoyed people: 'One minute you're like this, and then you want to do that. Now you don't want to do that. Which one it is?' That's how it felt. When all of us were together, Dave was controllable. You could talk to him and reason.

Dave finally said, 'I'm *definitely* going this time. You either come with me or you stay with the others.' I wish I had been strong enough to call his bluff and say, 'Go on then.' He might have said, 'Oh, maybe I'll think about that then,' or, 'If I'm on my own it might not be the same.' Equally, I didn't think, 'If I stay I will automatically become the lead singer of The Beat and Ranking Roger will run things.' You think about all these things years later. If I could replay it all I would know exactly how to play it and I would have stuck with the other guys. Instead, I kept thinking about what Dave was saying and how bands often outlive their time and wither away. The Specials had split up while 'Ghost Town' was at number one and Mick had formed Big Audio Dynamite after the 'Rock The Casbah' had made the Billboard Top 10. There were other bands too, and it seemed to be working for all of them. The Beat were on a high, so I said to myself, 'If we form a new band, that's a new thing.' So I went for it and finally said to Dave, 'Yeah, all right.'

While all this was being debated, 'Can't Get Used To Losing You' was released as a result of us splitting with Arista Records, along with a compilation album, *What Is Beat?* It was three years since we'd originally recorded the song for the first album. 'Can't Get Used To Losing You' sailed up the charts and was our first major hit since 'Too Nice To Talk To'. We were invited onto *Top of the Pops* for the first time in two years for the 1000th episode of the programme, presented by

Tommy Vance. At the BBC we met up with The Police, who were performing their fifth number one single, 'Every Breath You Take'. As usual we used the opportunity of live television to muck about a bit. Saxa had a balloon coming out of his instrument, Shuffle used a Paul McCartney-style Höfner violin bass, and I mimed with an electric guitar. I also recorded a special toast for the performance, name-checking three of my heroes:

Here we go now Iggy Pop, Lou Reed, David Bowie
everybody get together
Let's rock lets swing now sknenna, sknenna, sknenna.

It was something I used to do live and dated back to when the 2 Tone vocalists would make percussive sounds in a Jamaican style. Madness had *hip, hip, hip*. The Specials *he-he-he*. And I would always say *Iggy Pop, Iggy Pop, Iggy Pop*.

The 'best of' album climbed up to number ten, while 'Can't Get Used To Losing You' shot into the Top 5, warranting a second TV appearance on *Top of the Pops*. The record label would get the midweek chart position and bands would be expected to drop everything to pre-record *Top of the Pops* the day before transmission. It so happened that on this occasion I was on holiday in Ireland. Somebody managed to track me down by phoning the Pig and Whistle pub and passing on the urgent request. News travelled quickly in the village and a plane was chartered so I could race back to Birmingham to meet up with the band and travel down to the BBC. By then, we were used to such madness. Gary Davies introduced the band, and said, 'They told me they've just flown in from Birmingham to be with us tonight.'

Unbeknown to the rest of the band, Dave used the performance as an endgame. And so it was that The Beat performed for the last time on television. Towards the end of the song, Dave, dressed in a dinner suit which he'd borrowed from the BBC costume department, tossed his jacket over his shoulder and sauntered off stage, whistling. It was a farewell gesture. The whole thing was planned. Everyone thought it looked great but I knew what it meant. Dave was saying, 'It's the end of The Beat.' We both knew we were going to leave but at that point were still keeping it to ourselves. On the show you can see Andy and Shuffle sitting comfortably side by side on a drum riser smiling to one another, as if foretelling their new collaboration as Fine Young Cannibals, but I don't think they knew.

The next thing I knew we were booked to open for David Bowie on July 1, 2 and 3, 1983, at the Milton Keynes Bowl. It would be the last shows we would ever do as The Beat. In advance, Dave wrote a handwritten letter of resignation and I signed it, before he tucked it away for safekeeping. Before the first show, Bowie came into our dressing room and said, 'Hello, welcome to the tour. Have you got everything you need?' Saxa said, 'Where me Red Stripe? I want me Red Stripe.' Bowie popped out and we were all looking at Saxa opened-mouthed: 'Do know who that is?' He said, 'Me don't care who that is.' The next thing we knew Bowie came back in carrying a crate of beer: 'There you go boys.' Later, Saxa said he thought he was a waiter because he was wearing a black-and-white tuxedo. That was so human of Bowie. All my favourite pop stars have been approachable. You can have great conversations with them. At the end of the day they're just normal people. But at Milton Keynes I didn't hang out with Bowie. I thought it was best to give him space and peace. Everybody wanted a piece of him. I watched his show every night though. He had a great band with Earl Slick and Carlos Alomar on guitar. It was such a slick show. The musicianship was on par, really unlike us. Nonetheless, Bowie was really into our music and said we had a 'truly delicious sound' and 'it was a treat to watch us in action'.

On the last day of the three shows, Dave hand-posted our co-signed resignation through the letterbox of the band's management office in Handsworth. And then apparently, after the show, we came off stage and Bowie asked Dave if we wanted to support him on his upcoming nine-week tour across North America. I don't know how much truth is in that, but Dave has since said he tore back to Birmingham in the early hours of Monday morning and tried to retrieve the letter on his hands and knees with a stick. He didn't tell me that. If I had known, I would have said, 'You're too contradictory, Dave. How can I believe anything you say? You convinced me to leave the band and now you've changed your mind, again.' We could have gone to the office first thing on Monday morning and recovered the letter. I would have done that. As it was, the resignation letter was received but we never heard from the band. They must have been shocked, but nobody rang up and said, 'What the bloody hell are you doing?' or 'What's all this about?'

Richard Branson had been trying to sign The Beat to Virgin Records, and after the Bowie dates we met Branson three or four times. We basically said, 'The Beat's over. If you want to do the deal, do it with us two.' The Beat deal was changed and Dave and I signed to Virgin. We got a good deal. We had a lot of people to pay off. But if The Beat had had six months off and then come back to record a fourth album, we would have continued. The band split because of Dave and me. People made us believe we were important, and in all honesty, I went for the money and became a bread-head. We ended up with our heads in the clouds when we should have kept our feet on the ground. It was our fault. I accept my responsibility for that. I ruined something that meant so much to a generation.

Reflecting on what we had, The Beat was really a hippie band. Andy and Dave were proper college kids with long hair. It's the reason why everything flowed within the group as it did. It was very free flow. There was never any pressure from anyone towards anyone else. We all looked out for each other. The people were very cool and had good souls. I loved it. Maybe, the job was complete. Maybe we had done what we had to do, but it didn't feel like it. Andy, Shuffle, Everett and Saxa were loyal to The Beat. They were not snidey like Dave and me. We did it behind their backs. I felt so bad about that because as a band we had always spoken upfront about everything and out in the open. When everybody knows what's going on, people are cool. Dave and I broke that agreement.

As an act of desperation to keep the band in the pop market the record company released 'Ackee 1-2-3' in July 1983. It was another wrong move. The record flopped at number fifty-four. 'Ackee 1-2-3' was the kind of calypso music you heard in St Lucia. It got drilled in my ears when I was a youth. I wanted reggae and punk and pop and things my parents probably hated. 'End Of The Party' should have been the last single. Amongst all the new romantic crap it would have gone BOOF! But Shuffle vetoed it. It would have smashed it. It had so much feeling: nice build, great saxophones; and it told a story. It was a great love song.

The letter of resignation marked the official end point of The Beat. Saxa came on board with Dave and me and did some recording and touring with us. Everett, who was close with Saxa, sent his regards. There were no qualms between us. He was a very forgiving person and would have said, 'You've got to do what you've got to do. If that's what it takes then good luck to you.' Andy and Shuffle struggled for a while. It was hardly surprising; we had cut their circuit without any warning. Two years later they emerged as Fine Young Cannibals. It was the best thing they ever did. The first song I heard was 'Johnny Come Home'. It was brilliant. I heard the bass line, and thought, 'There's "Too Nice To Talk To" – part two.' I would have been proud to be part of that. It should have been a Beat tune with me and Dave Wakeling singing on it. There were a few rhythm tracks around similar to that, before we split up. Fine Young Cannibals showed us how The Beat should have been.

The first I spoke to Andy and Shuffle after the Bowie gigs was six years later. By then Fine Young Cannibals' second album, *The Raw And The Cooked*, had sold seven million copies. I met up with both of them in New York when they were megastars and I was a solo artist. They were pleased to see me. We went to an expensive sushi bar and I told them what I had been doing. I said, 'I didn't really want the band to split up but it was half my fault. I regret it. I didn't really want to leave but Dave was such a great talker and he convinced me.' Andy and Shuffle were millionaires and Fine Young Cannibals' success was way beyond what Dave and I had achieved, but they forgave me straight away. They were really cool about it. Shuffle said, 'Don't worry about it. No hard feelings. You were never the problem. We all knew that Dave could be difficult.'

We all changed in The Beat. But Dave didn't understand how much he was changing. It was a parting of personalities. It hurt the others. The many times when Dave asked me to go with him, and said, 'Right, this is it now. I'm leaving. If you're coming with me, come, or you stay' – that's what got to me: I knew I could sing and toast but I couldn't, all of a sudden, do all the lead vocals. I lost my self-esteem. I didn't have enough confidence. Like a lion I should have stood my ground, and said, 'Go on then. Fuck off.' I would have become the lead singer for The Beat: we would have been the Fine Young Cannibals with dub.

Part Five:
Can't Get Used To Losing You

Come And Join The Federation

General Public. Madonna. Groupies

G eneral Public was like a supergroup: a cool band mixing soul, ska and reggae.

After Dave and I left The Beat we immediately began a search to find local musicians from Birmingham. We found Micky Billingham and then Andy 'Stoker' Growcott, who would later engineer Ice Cube on the *Death Certificate* album. Both Micky and Stoker had been in Dexys Midnight Runners but in different line-ups, which bizarrely meant they had never played together before. Initially, I played bass and we invited Mick Jones to join us as a guest member on guitar. By then Mick was having success with Big Audio Dynamite but he was happy to come and rehearse with us. Dave and I had built a good friendship with Mick over the years and we gave him a free hand to do what he wanted. It was an honour to play with one of my heroes.

It was a really exciting time and we booked some demo time at Rockfield Studios in Monmouthshire. We were in the countryside by the river, we had a record deal and it felt like the future was in our hands. It was a great feeling. It was a magical place. This will sound crazy, but one evening, I could hear the sound of the dishwasher in the kitchen resonating through two separate closed-off rooms. Rather than the rumble of the machine, I heard a distinct bass line. I told Micky and hummed the melody I could hear to him, expecting him to say, 'You're bloody mad.' To my surprise, Micky said, 'No, this is what I hear,' and hummed a variation of the notes. We looked at each other in shock, and then said, 'Why don't we take the two and put them together?' We went straight into the rehearsal room and started getting it together. Shortly after, Dave came in, and said, 'What's going on here? This sounds good.' And so 'Dishwasher' was born, which we recorded as an instrumental track for the flip side of our debut single. Later, words were written and the song was retitled 'Burning Bright'.

During the initial General Public rehearsals it became obvious to everyone that I was struggling to play bass, sing and jump around all at the same time. I wouldn't accept it until one day I went round to Dave's house and Horace Panter was there, playing the bass. I went, 'You could have told me.' I'm sure Horace was very embarrassed about the situation but he was the right man for the bass job. My gripe was that Dave should have been more open and not gone behind my back, but I soon accepted the situation and Horace and Stoker formed a great rhythm section.

The name of the band, 'General Public', came from a noticeboard outside the Palace of Westminster, which read, 'This is private property and the General Public have no right to enter.' Dave saw it, and said, 'We should use that. General Public could be a dictator or the oppressed depending upon which way you look at it.' He was a smart thinker. We had a green-and-black logo designed, which gave it a military look, and two eyes. The eyes suggested Big Brother or perhaps, as some people commented, 'two machine guns'.

On the last Beat tour, Shuffle and I had bought Casiotone keyboards, one of the first portable players with a built-in drum machine. It was a robust, solid instrument and came in a small brown case. You could drop it on the floor and it wouldn't break. We were excited by the new technology and would sit down and spend hours together playing melodies. The Casiotone didn't have a record facility so you had to use a dictaphone to remember your ideas. It was another way of songwriting. I came up with numerous melodic ideas and once we got back off tour I recorded them on my home 4-track machine. Shuffle had given me his Fender precision bass guitar, which he had used to record the first album with, so I was able to lay down bass, drums and keyboard parts. It was enough to get simple ideas down. Amongst them were quite a few reggae tracks, a couple of pop tunes, a bit of calypso, a couple of love songs, two songs about joining the army – the first about what could happen to you; the second about the things which are done behind your back by people in charge – and one about the police called 'System Or Not?' The third verse was:

Always looking for the troublemaker
Good thinking, bad timing, you've got the wrong one,
Head man's plans are as bad as his thinking
Makes him worry he could be the next one

I played the tracks to Dave and he really liked them. They were written for The Beat, but due to the changed circumstances they found an outlet as General Public songs. 'System Or Not?' was renamed 'Limited Balance' and issued as the B-side of the single 'Tenderness'.

One of the first songs that we wrote was our debut single, 'General Public'. It was an anti-war song. I used a thesaurus and a lyric dictionary and between the two, I found a way to express myself. The first line I wrote was *come and join the federation*. I then used *-ation* as a rhyme scheme:

We could have communication
You can have your application
Be inside the battle station
Could this be your fascination
Look out for hallucinations
Stick right to the regulations
Must keep down the population

The chorus was:

That right you could act so badly
People never notice sadly
All the goings on behind the backs
Of men left well deserted

Dave said, 'We should go *general public uh uh, general public uh uh*,' and so that became the hook. I think you can tell a Ranking Roger song from a Dave Wakeling song, but Dave was a great person to write with. We had a vibe. We were hot. People all around the world loved our songs. It was a magic feeling. We had it in The Beat and again in General Public. We sang about the truth. We gave it everything we had and audiences knew we meant it. We could see in their faces at the end of a concert.

Whereas The Beat had been about rhythm, General Public was about getting hits with a soul and pop sound. I became the front man and did toasting, percussion and shared vocals with Dave to give him a break. I would always caution and say, 'Keep the roots. Keep the underground feel. Let's not be all-out commercial. We'll maybe be big this year but next year...'

Our first album, *All The Rage*, was recorded in Studio 1 at AIR Studios, which was owned by George Martin. It overlooked Oxford Street in central London. It was really big with a 3D soundscape. It was a top-of-the-range studio. I've never heard a better sound. On the first day of recording, while

Stoker was putting the drum tracks down, I went to get some air. I walked up to the reception, and asked the lady, 'Where can I find the gents and the refreshments?' All of a sudden everything went quiet. I looked up and saw Paul McCartney coming towards me. I hadn't fully computed who he was until he came up to me and said, 'All right Roger, how are you?' And shook my hand. I froze. I said, 'Paul, pleasure to meet you.' I was delighted to meet a Beatle and one of the greatest songwriters ever. I had travelled around the world and met pop stars – Joe Strummer, David Byrne, Sting – but they were kind of my peers and we were all riding a wave together. Paul McCartney was there before any of us. He was the original. It could only have been equalled by meeting Mick Jagger or Keith Richards.

I got a really warm vibe from Paul. He said, 'I really like your music.' I wanted to say, 'Wow! Which one's your favourite?' or, 'Well, that's probably because we ripped off "Beat" from The Beatles.' As it was, I was stuck for words. It was fantastic that he knew about us and was listening to what was out there. He said, 'We're in Studio 4, come in and have a listen. Feel free.' Later, I went in and George Martin was sat at the desk with Paul and an engineer. They were listening back to some stuff. I was thinking, 'Great production.' It was giving me ideas. George Martin was one of the greatest producers and I would have loved to have tapped his brain, but I was more concerned not to overstay my welcome. Paul and I got talking about how the music business was changing, and how all these new bands were coming in and what had happened with 2 Tone and then the new romantics. I remember saying, 'It's funny how fashion seems to change every six months.' I stayed for about twenty minutes, then I said, 'I better get back. Thank you for having me,' and shook all their hands. I wanted to stay longer because I was really interested in what they were producing but I got a bit nervous. It's one of the highlights of my life to have met a Beatle. Paul was as big as Elvis. And he was all right with me. He approached *me* and called my name. I didn't go up to him and say, 'Hello Paul, I'm Ranking Roger from The Beat.' That was something!

Despite the thrill of meeting a genuine star, in general, I hate the fame side of success. I enjoy making music and meeting people but when you go past a certain level of success it gets too extreme. Thankfully The Beat didn't attract tabloid interest and we generally kept to music-related publications. But the bigger you become the more open you are to criticism and everyone has their eye on you. Suddenly you're being written about in the gossip pages: 'Last night Ranking Roger was seen in a club with Madonna.' I remember getting a phone call from the *News of the World*: 'Is it true you slept with Madonna?'

During an earlier recording session at The Barge in Little Venice – owned by Richard Branson – I went to see Madonna do her debut UK showcase at the Camden Palace in north London [October 13, 1983]. Seymour Stein, the head of Sire Records, had introduced me to her in the States before she became a huge star. I found out she was a dancer at the Danceteria, my favourite club in New York, and I went to watch her a few times. The Danceteria was four floors of dance music with a different scene on every floor. Madonna was into The Beat and we chatted, had a couple of drinks together and got on. She was gorgeous but nothing happened. Then she came over to England to promote her debut single, 'Everybody', which I remember she played at the Camden Palace along with 'Burning Up' and 'Holiday' as a short introductory PA. When I listened to Madonna sing I used to close my eyes, and think, 'You sound like a black singer.' After the performance I went back with her to her hotel. There was definitely a little twinkle in her eye. But I have to be truthful and say nothing more happened. We kissed outside her room and then I left. It was a full-blown kiss with tongues but I was a gentleman, not least because there was a tour manager hanging around, and I thought, 'Best leave it at that.' Then all of a sudden there was rumour about us. People, were saying, 'What's going on with you and Madonna? Yeah, we know!' I took it in my stride. I was proud to have met her. The last time I saw anything of her was when I was with Special Beat. We played a sold-out show in Los Angeles and we knew she was coming. We came off stage, and somebody said, 'Madonna's here. She wants to come backstage and see you.' Neville and I were knackered, so I said, 'Just tell her to give us ten minutes so we can dry ourselves off and change.' I came out soon after but she was gone. Years later, I thought, 'You could have said, "Hello".' Regrettably, I've never seen her since.

I also had a massive crush on Susanna Hoffs from The Bangles. They opened for The Beat in North America in November and December 1982. I had the hots for her big time. There was something about her. She was so cute and innocent and talented. One night I managed to get into her room. It was a case of premature ejaculation. I wasn't even in her and everything was bursting. That's how hot the scene was. I had the utmost respect for Susanna and I reckon that if we had had a relationship I would have asked her for her hand in marriage. But as it was it was near the end of the tour and we went our separate ways. I've always held a flame for her – even more than Madonna. What a beautiful woman!

People always want to know about the sex, drugs and rock 'n' roll, and although Everett was interested in Debbi, The Bangles' drummer, in truth we weren't the type of band that went, 'Ooh, there's a support band full of girls. Who's going to end up with who?' The Specials were more like that. But we had a bit more decency in The Beat. We weren't wild dogs. We would pick and choose. 'Great, there's seven thousand lovely women here; look for the one who's got the character and the heart.'

During a gig, I'd laugh and joke around with girls in the audience. I'd get signals from body language and the way someone was dancing and looking at you. They'd know something was going on. You'd look at them and smile or blow a kiss to them, or say, 'This one goes to the young girl in the audience over there.' That's going to create something. If I liked the look of someone I'd go up to one of the roadies, and say, 'See that one? Tell her to come backstage after. Tell her we want to meet her.' He'd do it or tell one of the bodyguards to go and tell her. They'd say, 'Roger says...' or, 'Dave says, after the gig come backstage and meet the band, if you want to.' After the gig we'd meet up and chat. You could tell if they were interested. And then you would do it, in general, back at the hotel. It wasn't in the toilet or backstage. I had some decency. Although, saying that, I remember one gig. It was in either Boston or Chicago. There was a girl who had been to three or four of our gigs. I walked into the dressing room and she was there. I knew she was crazy over me. The last time we'd met we'd nearly done it but I'd had to leave because the band had a long-distance drive. But on this occasion she just looked me in the eye, I opened the toilet door and I pushed her in. And that was it: we started kissing and everything was coming off.

At the height of our popularity I had a girlfriend in every town. If it wasn't a fan in the audience it would be someone backstage you'd get talking to. Usually girls would come to two or three gigs before anything happened, but when it did it was hard to get rid of them. I was like, 'Okay, now we've slept with each other I'm not interested any more, really.' They'd turn up for the next year. It was awkward, particularly in the States. I pulled groupies but I was after the more sophisticated type. I didn't want just any girl. I wanted someone who had beauty and was intelligent too; personality. I usually went for the quiet types. If I fancied the arse off a girl it didn't mean that I necessarily slept with her. It wasn't like that. No one ever knows if it's just a one-night stand. You can presume it's for one night but if you like them you hope to see them again. But it doesn't mean you're going to have sex with them the next time you see them either. It wasn't like, 'Every time I come into your town you're my bird.' It might be someone else next time. 'Sorry, she got in first this time.'

We all played around. We were pop stars. By the end of The Beat it felt like The Beatles; I couldn't go anywhere without being recognised. I tried to stay calm and true to myself but we couldn't go anywhere. It was chaotic. I'd be walking down the road: 'Hey! You're that guy, Rodney English.' 'No, no. It's Ranking Roger from The English Beat.' All the girls that came backstage looked like top models. It was a different class. And as the singers, Dave and I got the most, although I got the nicer-looking ones because I went for a certain type. I was the wild one. But I have to say The Beat were a bunch of gentlemen. We treated women with respect. It wasn't just, 'All right. Next lot.' If I had a girlfriend she became my girlfriend on the road. You have to remember Saxa was there too; an elder man in the house. You had to respect that.

By the time General Public toured the States, the girl situation was getting incredible and more and more groupies appeared. I decided, 'Right, I'm going to have an American girlfriend and she comes everywhere with me so I'm left alone.' I had one for the West Coast and one for the East. Girls weren't really allowed on the coach; I used to have women fly to the next gig and the next – and then maybe once on the coach if it was a short journey – but the bus was the band's sanctuary. You don't invite anyone into your camp. You've got to make sure they're kosher. A girlfriend on the road always ended up in an argument. It's because you're in a place where there's five hundred girls in the audience who want you, and so they would naturally get jealous. Angela came to a few gigs. She had to stand there and watch the entire goings-on.

I lost my virginity when I was fourteen with a girl who was sixteen. She was my girlfriend but then my best mate slept with her, so I finished with her. I was angry with him, but then I thought, 'Nah man, you're my brethren. I'm not going to let a woman get in the way of our friendship.' I wasn't in love with her so life went on. It was the same with Dave and Dominique. You need to have a free mind to be a musician. You need to be able to focus on the music and not be looking after other people that are with you. It all nearly backfired once in England when I had my girlfriend with me and there were three other women I was seeing in Birmingham, and they were all in the audience. I had to go on stage and perform but I also had to go out to front-of-house and say hello to my girlfriend, because if I didn't things would kick off. I was terrified. You can imagine: 'I thought you were seeing me.'

Apart from me, Everett was a bad boy too. We were all bad boys but some more than others. It was inevitable, unless you brought your missus on tour. Girls would be coming up and going, 'Come here,' and showing you their tits and everything. I was thinking, 'I can't.' That's what it was like in the early Eighties. Everybody was shagging everybody else, until suddenly there was the government's 'Don't Die of Ignorance' campaign. Overnight it stopped. AIDS had a massive impact on casual sex. I was promiscuous. I now realise I could have caught HIV. People weren't taking precautions. There was a lot of bareback riding. Nowadays, I look at it totally different. The prettiest girl in the world could come into my dressing room and I might say, 'Oh, you're pretty,' but that's as far as it would go.

When General Public recorded at the Manor in Oxfordshire, a pretty woman from MTV came to interview Dave, and the next thing I knew they were upstairs. I was like, 'How dare you do that with your wife here', but it turned out she knew what was going on. All sorts of shenanigans were going on. The whole thing was sordid and soon after, Dave and Dominque divorced.

When I first met Dave I suspected he was bisexual. He never tried anything on with me but he had gay friends who I knew and they were all right. It didn't matter to me if he was gay or not. It's what's in a person's heart that counts. It's about humility and brotherhood. I accepted gay people a long time ago. The Beat spoke about equal rights and gay rights and women's rights and black rights. It was all seen as equal. We took it all in and accepted it. Years later, Dave came out and confirmed he was bisexual on a live American TV show. Blockhead was also gay but nobody knew at the time. It had been more than a decade since the Sexual Offences Act 1967 decriminalised homosexual acts in private between two men, but it was still difficult for many men to come out in public.

Mum was the first person I knew who accepted gay people. She had gay friends who would come to the house and they'd have a laugh. In St Lucia, there was a gay guy who I was friends with. He used to get grilled when he walked through town because he used to mince and wear make-up. My sisters thought he was hilarious. He'd say to me, 'A dread who's not grilling me!' I'd say, 'But I'm an English dread.'

Eat To The Beat

Drugs. Spirituality

When *All The Rage* was released in 1984, we opened for Queen at the RDS Simmons Hall in Dublin, the NEC in Birmingham and four nights at Wembley Arena on the Works Tour. The gigs came through management. It was a very unusual call. We had to go on soon after doors had opened to an audience that didn't know who General Public were. It was hard to push a rock audience but they seemed to like us by the end of the set. Brian May was a really nice guy. On the first night I went up to the side of the stage while he was working on his amps and sounds, and he was like, 'All right, Roger, welcome.' I can't knock that. He had time for me but he was the only one. I only got nods from the others and I never met Freddie Mercury. I didn't even get eye contact with him. No one could get near him. Swivelhead-looking guys always surrounded him so I didn't even try and approach him.

I would have liked to at least shaken his hand, and said, 'Thank you.' Queen were gods, as far as their fans were concerned, but they were not really my kind of music. I liked 'Bohemian Rhapsody'. It was clever, but I was more into David Bowie and Lou Reed.

On tour, Dave and I employed a bodyguard called John Richards. He was a black belt in karate and he made us do martial arts. He was strict and every day after soundcheck we had to do half an hour of exercises before we could eat. It kept us supple and fit. In a bizarre contradiction, during this time I took acid for the first time while we were in America. I was with Digby Cleaver, who had been Mick Jones' roadie in The Clash. We stopped at a 76 Truck Stop and Digby gave me half a tab. He said, 'Don't tell anyone because I'll be fired.' I said, 'I don't normally do this. You don't tell anyone.' Twenty minutes later the band coach pulled up at the diner and the rest of the group came in to order food. Digby and I burst out in hysterics. Nobody had a clue what we were laughing at, not even us, I suspect. It got so bad we had to go back to the bus without any dinner.

I've never been that interested in hard drugs. I've always been what I call a 'Bunsen burner'; I burn weed. It's the most natural drug you can get – after all, it is a herb. I started smoking weed when I joined The Beat and quickly learnt how to roll a joint. Drugs were everywhere if you wanted them. Pubs used to smell of weed. Growing up, I saw it all around me, particularly at sound system dances. Smoke was everywhere but nobody said anything. Even when the police came to say, 'Can you keep the noise down we've had complaints,' they turned a blind eye to the marijuana. The system tells you, 'If you take drugs they will make you go out and mug old ladies and become violent and burgle people's houses to fund your habit.' Or, 'If you smoke weed you will end up smoking heroin and become a crack addict.' It doesn't go like that. I've been burning for forty years and I have never laid my hand on one person in all that time. I've never stolen from anybody. I've never mugged anybody. I've never caused trouble. It's a myth. Nowadays you have skunkweed, which is ten times stronger than anything we used to burn. I prefer Jamaican weed because it's natural. Saxa always used to say, 'You must put it in a pipe and don't use tobacco.' Most of the time Saxa smoked tobacco in his pipe but other times it was weed. I would think, 'I've read about dope. I've seen other people do it. I've heard a million songs about smoking.'

Harder drugs were a different matter. I saw what they did to the punks; some died of heroin overdoses, others took too much speed and ended up in mental institutions. The drugs changed in The Beat during the American leg of the *Wha'ppen?* tour. I kept seeing these guys dressed in smart black suits and ties. They looked like CIA or FBI agents. I'd see them hanging around backstage and then they'd vanish. I ignored them until near the end of the tour, when I heard a rumour that the band owed some Mafia-type guys over $5,000 for cocaine and other drugs. I knew some of the guys took powders, from time to time, but I didn't know how much. They knew I wasn't interested. They had all been using speed and cocaine before I was even in the band so I was always aware of it being around. By the time we got to California I confronted a member of the crew and was told that there was a drug debt and these guys were going to do people over unless they got paid. They were serious. Eventually, I was told they were paid off: 'Forget about it. It's all right.' I was like, 'What do you mean they've just been paid off? Who are they?' One of the roadies said, 'We ordered all this cocaine and different things in New York and these guys followed us.' I was like, 'Bloody hell!' I was really shocked. I'd overheard snippets of conversation during the tour, and the words 'angel dust' had been used. I knew that was really serious. Maybe people were just trying it once because they were in America, but it was dangerous. I was surprised but very glad none of the band ended up as serious drug addicts.

Heroin was never in The Beat, unlike The Clash, who had an acute problem with heroin. Topper was the main culprit. I'm glad we never had those kinds of problems. In The Beat it was weed and coke. I never really saw it because I was so anti-drugs. It mashes up your head and eats out your skull. The others wouldn't do it in front of me because I would have something to say. I started saying, 'Ah, the devil's dandruff.' They didn't like it being called that. If you put marijuana into the equation we were all into some kind of drug, but it didn't affect my relationships within the band. In America, you were asked all the time, 'Hey, you wanna try a line?' I'd say, 'No, I'm just a Bunsen burner.' Once we got to Holly-weird and Collie-fornia, as I call them, cocaine was everywhere. It was coming from record company types and executives, as well as the audience and the tag-alongs. It's up to each man to choose. For me, 'No, means no.' There was no pressure because I was adamant where I stood. I knew I wanted to be alive when I was sixty. I had a wise head.

I now have to contradict myself because, truth be told, I took cocaine twice. It was around the time of 'Tears Of A Clown'. Chrysalis was having a big party for Blondie to celebrate their new album, *Eat To The Beat*, and we had been asked to play as part of the event. The launch was in a massive hall in London; the tables were laid out all posh and because it was near to Christmas there was a thirty-foot tree brushing the ceiling. I went backstage and I met up with some music industry people. Everybody was taking cocaine, and somebody said, 'Would you like a line?' I was naïve. I knew what it was, but I was on such a high that we were playing for Blondie and imagining what it might lead to, so I agreed. This guy chopped out two lines and handed me a rolled bank note, and I snorted both lines. At first, it made my teeth tingle and then I was feeling my gums with my tongue and they were numb. It felt like an anaesthetic at the dentist. I was sniffing but everything was fine until about ten minutes later, when I went back out to the hall and was saying hello to everybody. What I didn't realise was that cocaine makes you talk and talk and talk. And then suddenly BANG! I walked straight into the Christmas tree. The whole thing fell down and crashed to the ground and baubles and decorations went flying everywhere. I was so embarrassed. I didn't know what to do. Luckily people were saying, 'It's all right. Don't worry.' On top of that I still had to perform. I can't imagine what I sounded like. Usually after the first drum hit I'm running up and down the stage, but I had to stay still and do everything slowly. I was trying to dance but I felt like Robotman. I imagine my singing wasn't much better; I certainly couldn't tell you if it was in tune or not. It was a very weird experience.

The second time I took cocaine was in 1995, by which point I was supposed to be a responsible parent. Pato Banton and I had recorded 'Bubbling Hot', and it reached number fifteen in the UK chart. We were invited onto *Top of the Pops* on two separate occasions and I was ecstatic. After the first recording I came back to Birmingham and met up with some friends. One of them said, 'Let's do a trip.' I'd never done acid before but I trusted these people. I had read that if you take hallucinogenic drugs you should be amongst people who are well-minded and have good hearts, so if anything happens they know what to do and how to deal with the situation. I took the tab and it was the strangest thing. It was really strong acid and we stayed up all night tripping. One guy was being weird and trying to play on our weaknesses, but everybody else was having a good time. I didn't have hallucinatory visions, as such, but colours became brighter and more vivid. I remember seeing intense yellows with a haze around them. It was a minimal experience. In the morning, we went to a house in Small Heath and I had some cocaine to stay up because I didn't want to go to sleep. It took me weeks to recover. It wasn't the comedown as much as getting over what I'd done, and I didn't feel myself again for several weeks.

In many ways, taking drugs is part of your spiritual journey, and for me one of the great influences on life has been *The Urantia Book*, which was given to me as a gift when I was thirty-four. It's a spiritual and philosophical book that has opened my mind and soul – in fact, my whole persona – and has made me feel so spiritual at times that I find it hard to bear and I want to give so much love out to people. Around 1911, a man in Chicago, who has remained anonymous, was having dreams and speaking incredible spiritual words whilst he was asleep. His wife couldn't understand their meaning, and when the man woke he had no memory of what he had said. His wife approached two local physicians, Lena and William Sadler, who listened to the man when he was in this subconscious state and recorded what he was saying. They did it for over twenty years and then collated the material and published it in 1955 as *The Urantia Book*.

I was at home one day and there was a ring on the doorbell. It was Pato Banton. I said, 'Come in, man. I haven't seen you in ages.' He had just come back from a successful American tour and stood on the doorstep with a big smile across his

face. He said, 'You're into UFOs aren't you?' I said, 'Yeah.'
He said, 'You're into angels?' I said, 'Yeah, I believe in angels
and God and all that.' He said, 'I better come in then.' And he
handed me *The Urantia Book*. I was absorbed by it and started
going to meetings above a new age bookshop called Zen, in
Brindley Place. As many as thirty people would be there and
we would each read passages from the book and discuss them
together. Once I went to an informal gathering in a very posh
house in Oxford and there was a whole mix of people there;
from rich to poor to high court judges. One guy I spoke to was
an atheist who worked for the BBC and he had been reading
the book for over thirty years. That told me something. It's so
ahead of its time it will take five hundred years for mankind to
fully recognise the depth of its writing and wisdom concerning
science, nature and the planet.

The Urantia Book is a fascinating, amazing read and has
become a focal point for my life. It has given me a spiritual
understanding of people and taught me how to recognise the
difference between those who are genuine and those who
seek to abuse you. When I am confronted by something, I
say to myself, 'How would God deal with this?' I had always
believed in God but I was suspicious of priests. As I child,
I was confirmed and took Communion, but I would ask
questions of the church, like, 'All right then, if God made
us, who made God? No one can create themselves... that's
stupid.' I then became really interested in the unexplained;
anything we didn't have answers for – the psychic; UFOs;

ghosts – and I buy *The Unexplained: Mysteries of Mind, Space & Time* magazine every month. It gave me the understanding to look beyond religion and realise that I was a truth-seeker. It has been a lifetime's dedication.

The only way to find truth is to be humble. I don't see this 'pop star' bullshit. After I appeared on *Top of the Pops* for the first time, people's perception of me changed. I used to be able to cross the old Bull Ring on foot in ten minutes. Once 'Tears Of A Clown' went in in at number six, the same walk would take an hour and a half. I refused to travel in taxis or have limousines. I'd get on the local bus and everyone would recognise me. Even after we'd had four or five hits, I would still take the bus to rehearsals. People would say, 'Get a car. You're seventeen now!' I'd be like, 'No. This is the way I do it. You want me to change overnight; that's when the head's gone and you become a diva.' I saw it in others around me and I saw people get away with murder. I knew that if I succumbed to the temptations I would lose whatever gift I had. I came from punk. We were anti-establishment. We were anti-flash cars and five star hotels and all the airs and graces that go with that lifestyle. Rejecting that is the mark of a true human (although, I did eventually concede to buying a little Mini); all the old musicians were like that.

I once went to Ireland and met Noel Redding, the bass player in The Jimi Hendrix Experience. Noel lived in Dunowen House in Ardfield with his girlfriend and I often stayed with them. He had a lovely house, with so many gold and platinum discs on the walls. It was surrounded by four acres of land. Noel deserved more. He should have had a sixteen-bedroom mansion and a hundred acres of land. He was such a nice man. He was grounded and very soon we bonded. I ended up playing drums with him a couple of times in the local pub in Clonakilty. Noel would start a riff, and then we'd jam. He told me stories about what went on in the Sixties and how they were all ripped off. He said Hendrix was safe; a cool guy. When I was in Special Beat, Noel introduced me to Mitch Mitchell. I was like, 'I've met two of The Jimi Hendrix Experience now!' I just missed Jimi!

Never You Done That

Nelson Mandela. Beat reunion

In 1984, Jerry Dammers invited me and Dave Wakeling to sing on a new song he had written about Nelson Mandela. I had learnt about the apartheid regime in South Africa at school and through the Socialist Workers Party. Mandela was the subject of many reggae records and I recognised him as an African freedom fighter with an admirable non-violent stance. Elvis Costello produced the record at AIR Studios, and when I read Jerry's lyrics, and particularly the opening line *shoes too small to fit his feet* I was shocked. Musically, it was a great tune with a fantastic hook line and very much had the feel of a calypso song. Afrodiziak – Caron Wheeler, Claudia Fontaine and Naomi Thompson – had already laid down some beautiful harmonies and we added some parts to complement their rich voices. '(Free) Nelson Mandela' was a message song and made pop music history when it charted by bringing the plight of Nelson Mandela and the African National Congress into millions of households across the country. One song in half a million has that kind of impact on people, and it meant the world to contribute to its success.

The only time I ever sang '(Free) Nelson Mandela' outside of the recording studio was on *The Tube* when we sang our harmonies, stood beside Elvis Costello, with Jerry's newly formed Special AKA. It was an odd experience, not least because we had to rush over, having just made our television debut as General Public performing 'Never You Done That' and 'General Public'. We were wearing our new futuristic space-age look, which had been designed for us by Exile in Manchester, and I also dyed my hair to look like how it was when I was a punk, with a blonde streak. By now I was quite familiar with wearing make-up, which I had started using when we did 'Can't Get Used To Losing You' on *Top of the Pops*. Everybody wore make-up in the Eighties. New romantic bands had become popular and they all looked like women. It was part of the fashion. Make-up artists would say, 'Your forehead looks shiny on the camera so you need to use a touch of powder.' First it was to take the gloss off, and then it was, 'Oh well, make me look handsome, then!' In some situations it gave the wrong impression. We did a shoot with David Bailey. He really liked me. He said, 'You have the most amazing smile. I could take pictures of you all day.' I was wearing make-up and mascara and he made me look really good. But I chose the frames where I looked mean. Anyway, I digress. Four years after recording '(Free) Nelson Mandela', a 70th Birthday Tribute was staged at Wembley Stadium, with an all-star ensemble performing, including Dire Straits, Eurythmics, Whitney Houston and UB40, and Jerry's anthem was performed as the finale. Dave and I weren't invited. I guess it was a new chapter in pop music by then.

Charity records were all-pervasive in the mid-Eighties, and in the wake of Live Aid, I contributed to an old Pioneers song, to raise money for the famine areas of Ethiopia, Eritrea and Sudan. 'Starvation' was recorded at Madness' newly built studio, Liquidator, and Jerry Dammers was once again at the helm and brought together a vast array of musicians from the 2 Tone family to perform on the record. The roll call included Ali and Robin Campbell from UB40, Brad, Lynval and Dick Cuthell from The Specials, Bedders and Woody from Madness, and the original Pioneers, Jackie Robinson, Sydney Crooks and George Agard. I came in to do some backing vocals, and Jerry suddenly said, 'Will you do the toast?' I was thrown into the deep end. I sat down and wrote some lyrics. People knew Jerry was un-together, but when he got-it-together, he was a genius.

Even though General Public was taken seriously and made good money, ultimately we were too much of a pop band. The first album was brilliant but the second record was disappointing. Between the releases of the two records I began to have doubts and regrets about leaving The Beat. Dave and I had been in two bands together and spent the best part of ten years together as musical partners. It was more than some marriages. I began to lose interest and looked for work with others, like the Blue Riddim Band. We did a tune about Nancy Reagan, 'America & Russia/Selective Service System (Nancy Goes To Moscow)', and the twelve-inch has since become a collector's item. In the end I just left General Public and went back to live in Moseley. In many ways, I had missed out on my teenage years. From the ages of sixteen to twenty-two I was constantly on the road. When all my mates were going out to nightclubs I was on the other side of the world. I was lucky. I could so easily have left school with no qualifications, signed on the dole, and ended up in prison. If I had to do it again, in this day and age, I wouldn't get as far as the top of the road. Things are so sewn up and tight, and the chances I had are long gone. Back then, you could move between different posses and create something. I took the risk and went for it.

With my departure, General Public disbanded. Dave remarried and moved to California. He worked for Greenpeace as a Special Projects Director for a few years, protecting whales and coordinating protestors handcuffing themselves to railroads to prevent nuclear transportation. I thought that was the end of our working relationship. Then, in 1994, Ralph Sall got in contact. He was putting the music together for a new film called *Threesome*, based on the college-day memories of the writer and director, Andrew Fleming. Ralph was a General Public fan and asked Dave and I if we would record The Staple Singers' soul classic 'I'll Take You There'. I went over to the States and the track worked really well. Sony Records backed the project, released it as a single, and it got to number twenty-two on the Billboard chart and number one on the dance chart. As a result, Epic Sony signed General Public for $1 million. Initially the offer was in the region of $200,000, until we became involved with a loud-mouthed manager, Jeff Kwatinetz. He was a man who could get things done, and would go on to manage Michael Jackson. Jeff renegotiated our deal up to $750,000, and once the extras were included through the recording process, it reached the $1 million mark.

The newly formed General Public recorded an album called *Rub It Better*, and we even brought the tapes back to Birmingham to record Saxa because he was too ill to travel. From *Rub It Better* we released a single that I had written called 'Rainy Days', but during a promotional interview with an influential music industry newspaper, Dave said something derogatory about the record label, along the lines of 'the people at Sony didn't know what they were doing'. Three days later we were dropped, without a reason. It is difficult to accept that the two events were coincidental. It was all there for us on a plate. 'Rainy Days' was a catchy tune, in my opinion, and a potential hit. By the mid-Nineties, America was ready and not only accepting but embracing reggae artists like Shaggy and Buju Banton. It was my chance. Once you have sold four million albums then you can voice your opinion. You certainly don't beforehand, when your success relies on the backing of your record company.

By then, Dave was drinking quite a bit, and I'd had enough. I kept on threatening to leave but he didn't believe me. I didn't

NEVER YOU DONE THAT

need the constant bullshit and just wanted to carry on with my own music and be happy again. So I left General Public and the same night joined Big Audio Dynamite. General Public had played the second of two nights at the House of Blues in Los Angeles, both of which had sold out; 4,000 people. I didn't even say goodbye to Dave. I just said, 'I'm out of here.' He could see I was in a bad way but I grabbed my stuff from the dressing room and walked off. A friend, Dr James, was waiting for me outside in a jeep and we drove down Sunset Boulevard to the Whiskey a Go Go on Sunset Strip. Mick had already invited me to join him on stage for the fourth number but I was running late. The club was heaving and as I was trying to get through the crowd I could hear the tune I was meant to be on. I was thinking, 'I've got to get to the mic before the instrumental.' People were going, 'It's Ranking Roger,' and pushing me forward. I got on stage and picked up the mic just in time for my toast. I did three numbers and that was the beginning of my next eighteen months, as a member of Big Audio Dynamite.

There have been several attempts to reunite the original line-up of The Beat. The first was by VH1 for *Bands Reunited*. Richard Blade, who was a hip DJ I knew from Los Angeles, flew over from the States to do an interview with me, and halfway through the conversation a camera crew arrived. At the time, I was in a band called Twist & Crawl, with Everett and Blockhead, performing mostly Beat tunes. In front of a live camera, I was asked if I would agree to a Beat reunion. I agreed and the filmmakers asked if I would contact Everett. I set up an interview but I didn't tell him the cameras were going to be there. Everett cussed me at first but then was nearly in tears. He loved the idea of The Beat reforming. Off camera, we tried to get everybody together to have a chat, in a café. Andy and Shuffle were reluctant and said they could do without the hassle. They are both private people and don't like being in the public eye. I understood that. VH1 didn't.

Shortly after, *Mojo* magazine persuaded Dave and I to reform the band for a one-off concert at the Royal Festival Hall on February 7, 2002. Again, Shuffle wouldn't do it. We had a couple of rehearsals in Birmingham, but then Andy said, 'I don't think I can do this. But I'm going to get you the best PA and lights in London.' I didn't question it. The gig was a great thing to do. People were so happy to see us play, many who thought The Beat would never reform, and some had travelled from Europe and as far as America to see us. There was so much excitement in the hall. Everybody knew the songs, although Dave forgot the lyrics to 'Big Shot' on the third verse. I know how that feels. It happens. I was proud it went so well and had such a brilliant feeling during the gig. The night before, we did a warm-up in a small pub in Birmingham called the Anchor, which was owned by Twist & Crawl's guitar player. The place was heaving and there was queues all the way down the stairs and out the venue. We got on stage and it was packed solid. The room was bouncing and you could see plaster and dust coming down from above the chandeliers. The gaffer thought the ceiling was going to collapse. It was heavy. That was the night Murphy first came on stage as 'Ranking Junior'. I was so proud. Then at the Festival Hall the following night, in front of 3,000 people, he lapped it up. It was short, sharp and sweet. The audience loved it and it showed it was still possible to keep The Beat going.

Post-gig, I was sure we would continue as The Beat. I already had some small gigs booked with Everett as Twist & Crawl and we invited Dave to do a handful of them with us, which he happily agreed to. He was on the drink at the time and he'd come on stage in a bawdy mood. I lived with it for one or two nights and then asked him to tone it down. I don't swear when I'm on stage so I won't have it with others. I didn't want to be on stage with somebody taking the piss out of the numbers. He would say things like, 'This is Roger and Dave's "*Shave* It For Later".' I didn't want to hear it. It came to a head at a free outdoor gig at Birmingham University for kids and families. Dave came on and was uncontrollable. We came off and before the encore I had a go at him, and then said, 'You're not going back on.' We went on without him and did 'Mirror In The Bathroom'. He went absolutely mad but I had had enough. That was the last time we performed together. After that I carried on as The Beat in the UK and Dave formed The English Beat in America. The next time I saw him was in 2017, when his band came to Birmingham and I performed on stage with him.

I know fans would like to see Dave and I work together again, but I've put so much hard work into my version of The Beat. I've been doing it for over fifteen years. I've gone from playing to a hundred people in 2002 to a sold-out night in front of 3,000 people at the Roundhouse in 2017. I'm in a difficult situation. Dave has spent all these years touring in America as The English Beat – playing to smaller and smaller audiences – and while my band sounds, to my ears, like the original Beat, his version sounds like a Las Vegas karaoke version. If I went over to the States his band would hate me because I'd make them play the songs to sound like how they were originally performed. Dave sent me some lyrics in 2018 with a note saying, 'Here you are. Try this to one of your tunes. I don't want anything for it.' I may send him something back one day. I know he would like my toasting on one of his records, but I'm a bit reserved because then Dave can claim it as the 'proper' new Beat album. Instead, we have both released our own versions of The Beat.

In 2016, I put out *Bounce* as The Beat featuring Ranking Roger, and in 2018 Dave reclaimed the name The English Beat for his album *Here We Go Love*. Then in January 2019, I released a second album, *Public Confidential*. It's the closest record I've made to the feel of The Beat's debut record, forty years earlier. I wanted to go back to our original sound one more time: listen to the single 'Who's Dat Looking', and you will hear a clear lineage to 'Mirror In The Bathroom'. I can now move forward with a clean palate and incorporate the ideas of Saffren, Leon and Murphy to create a futuristic vision of The Beat. My plan is for it to be like a Birmingham Massive Attack.

After The Beat reunion in 2002, many of our peers reformed, amongst them The Specials, The Selecter and The Police. To be able to hear those bands again is a good thing, but there is a fine line between offering something new wishing they'd left their past alone. But at least audiences are getting something, rather than nothing. Reforming bands is about keeping a legacy alive. It's okay doing all the old hits and getting the crowd going, but what decides your future is new songs. Music to me has never been about fame or a million-selling album. I just want integrity and to remain underground. It's never been about the money. It's what you bring to the community. What you do with your actions. I look for honesty and integrity in people, not qualifications. I have learnt from the University of Life. I know that if I was put out on the street tomorrow I could survive. I've been out there. I've lived the stories. 'Don't pump yourself up too much,' that's my thing. 'Be prepared because anything could change at any time.' It sounds paranoid, but I'm a person who is aware and ready. Today, I have my own version of The Beat. I close my eyes and I sing, and it sounds just like the original band. It's got the vibe. It's got the flavour. The crowds love it. I am as satisfied now as I would be had it been all the original guys. Over the past twenty years I've made The Beat mine. In the UK we're loved again. I'm playing the music I love and I think it shows. That's why I still do it. It's coming from the heart. I still believe in the songs and I'll do it as long as I can. It's what I've done all my life. It's what I do. I'm the cool entertainer. The only thing that would make me stop doing it would be illness or war. It's a compulsion. I Just Can't Stop It.

END OF THE PARTY
Postscript

Days after completing the last page of this book, and with the prophetic assertion, 'The only thing that would make me stop doing it would be illness,' Roger discovered he had cancer.

Roger was at home and suddenly collapsed losing the use of his right arm and some speech. He was rushed to hospital and told he had suffered a stroke. Two tumours were discovered on Roger's brain which necessitated immediate surgery. Then, during the procedure, doctors learnt Roger also had lung cancer.

The timing could not have been worse. Having toured Europe and in Australia on a double-headline tour with The Selecter in 2018, America awaited. It would have been Roger's first tour of the US with The Beat since 1983. 'What was going to happen in America?' Roger reflected. 'There was some reason why I shouldn't go. Do I believe in fate? You never know. I believe what's meant to happen will happen so

I must believe in fate. It's a shame because we would have whopped it.'

Roger had never been to hospital as an adult, but in December 2018 he was admitted to Queen Elizabeth Hospital Birmingham where both tumours were successfully removed and he was placed on a two year programme of Immunotherapy. The instruction from his National Health medical staff was to rest. 'Once you can keep your hand up for ninety minutes, with a microphone in it, we'll let you sing again.'

Roger was defiant. 'I know I will be back. I've just got to be positive and get myself sorted out. I want to be jumping up on stage and having fun. That's what people expect of me.' Roger was determined to play a part in the fortieth anniversary of 2 Tone. His positivity was testament to the thirteen-year-old boy who had a vision of his future role in life as an entertainer. The last time I spoke to Roger was in February 2019 when I suggested that he was being incredibly brave in the face of such a traumatic turn of events in his life. He responded, 'I must be brave because I'm not scared.' Before adding a message for his fans, 'I will survive this. But if you want you can say your prayers for me.'

It was a blessing that did not foresee the cancer aggressively returning. Despite a shock of radiation treatment, Roger's health rapidly deteriorated. Amongst the many visitor's at the Queen Elizabeth, where Roger was readmitted, was Pauline Black. 'It was made even more poignant being St. Patrick's Day,' she said. 'I remembered very clearly the truly awesome show that The Beat and The Selecter put on in Dublin at the Olympia Theatre just one year ago to the day. Roger was so full of life and bursting with energy and joy during the "Enjoy Yourself" encore. And now, here we are. I have been laid low in spirits ever since.'

Roger's final wish was to be at home, in Bearwood. And there, surrounded by family, Roger died on Tuesday 26 March, 2019, aged fifty-six.

Among the tens of thousands of tributes that followed a line from *Hamlet*, shared by Pauline, captured the air:

Good night sweet prince: And flights of angels sing thee to thy rest!

Daniel Rachel

GIGOGRAPHY

This is an attempt to compile a listing of the live shows The Beat played between 1979 and 1983, alongside significant key dates. The publishers would welcome any additional information that could be used to amend or update this information for future published editions.

1979
March
31 Matador (supporting Dum Dum Boyz)
Bournebrook, Selly Oak

April
Dates with UB40

June
June–September Mercat Cross residency, Birmingham
Moseley with Au Pairs
Summerfield Park with UB40
Aston University (supporting John Peel)

August
Cascade, Shrewsbury (supporting The Selecter)

September
Blackpool (supporting The Selecter)
Sheffield
23 Nashville (supporting The Selecter)
The Bridgehouse, Canning Town (supporting The Selecter)

October
4 Canterbury College of Art (supporting The Selecter)
13 Electric Ballroom (supporting The Selecter and the
   Mo-dettes)
Underworld Club, Birmingham
24 Record Peel Session

November
8 Rock Garden, Covent Garden
11 Lyceum, London (supporting The Teardrop Explodes and
   The Human League)
12 The Bridgehouse, Canning Town
16 University of Surrey with the John Peel Roadshow
17 Hope & Anchor R 'n' B Festival, Islington

December
Tiffany's, Coventry (with UB40)
9 Lyceum, London (supporting The Selecter and UB40)
14 Stroud

19 Eric's, Liverpool

20 Tiffany's, Coventry (supporting The Specials)

21 Castle Pub, Windsor

1980

January

4 The Porterhouse, Nottingham

Cascade, Shrewsbury (day after recording 'Hands Off...
   She's Mine')

19 Newcastle University

23 Top Rank, Birmingham

24 Stateside Centre, Bournemouth

25 Polytechnic, Brighton

26 Electric Ballroom, Camden (UB40 plus Akrylykz
   featuring Roland Gift)

27 Lyceum, London with The Selecter and Secret Affair
   (Capital Radio, children's charity gig)

February

3 Tiffany's, Coventry

7 Pavilion, Bath

10 Locarno, Bristol

21 Civic Hall, Guildford

22 Pavilion, Bath

23 Queensway Hall, Dunstable

27 Top Rank, Birmingham (+ afternoon show)

March
1 Kinema, Dunfermline
2 Tiffany's, Glasgow
3 Tiffany's, Edinburgh
30 University of East Anglia, Norwich

May
Twelve-date European tour:
10 Paradiso, Amsterdam
Hanover, Germany
Lyon, France
24 Friars, Aylesbury
25 Top Rank, Brighton
26 Top Rank, Sheffield
27 Mayfair, Newcastle
28 Assembly Rooms, Derby
29 Corn Exchange, Cambridge
30 University of East Anglia, Norwich
31 Arts Centre, Poole

June
2 Tiffany's, Coventry
3 Victoria Hall, Stoke Hanley
6 Top Rank, Cardiff
8 Brunel Rooms, Swindon
9 Winter Gardens, Malvern
10 Grand Pavilion, Withernsea

12 Unity Hall, Wakefield

13 University, Leicester

15 Locarno, Bristol

17 Locarno, Portsmouth

19 King George's Hall, Blackburn

20 Middleton Civic Hall, Manchester

21 Russell Club, Manchester

24 Hammersmith Palais, London

27, 28 Top Rank, Birmingham

June

22 Hortens Festivalen, Norway

July

27 *Rockpalast*, Germany

TV Holland

August

10 Hippodrome, Le Touquet, FR

12 Parking du Yachting, Cabourg, FR

14 Palais de la Beaujoire, Nantes, FR

16 Chapiteau Parking du Stade, Royan, FR

18 Parc de Sports d'Aguilerra, Biarritz, FR

22 Arenes, Beziers, FR

24 Palais des Sports, Grenoble, FR

All dates with The Police, XTC and UB40

September

3 Record Peel Session

7 Music Hall, Cleveland

8 Riviera Theatre, Chicago

10 So. Illinois University, Carbondale

11 University of Illinois, Champaign

12 Uptown Theater, Kansas City

13 Night Moves, St Louis

14 The Orpheum, Memphis

15 Agora, Atlanta

17 Empire Theatre, Richmond

18 Peabody's, Virginia Beach

19 George Washington University, Washington, DC

20 Painters Mill, Baltimore

21 Yale University, New Haven

23 Ritz, Long Island

24 Palladium, New York

25 Rutgers University, New Brunswick

26 Capitol Theatre, Passaic

27 Orpheum Theatre, Boston

28 Tower Theater, Upper Darby

All dates supporting The Pretenders

30 Boston

October

2 Montreal

3 Ottawa

4 Toronto

8 Philadelphia

9 New York

10 Emerald City, Cherry Hill, NJ (filmed for *Dance Craze*)

11 Santa Cruz

12 San Francisco

15, 16 Los Angeles

17, 18 Greek Theatre, Los Angeles (supporting
   Talking Heads)

19 Arlington Theatre, Santa Barbara (supporting
   Talking Heads)

20 Palladium, Hollywood (supporting Talking Heads)

22 Zellerbach Hall, UC Berkeley

23, 24 Warfield Theatre, California

26 Aragon Ballroom, Chicago

27 Oriental Theatre, Milwaukee

28 Northrop Auditorium, Minneapolis

30 Masonic Auditorium, Detroit

31 John Carroll University Gym, University Heights

November

2, 3 Radio City Music Hall, New York

4 Capitol Theatre, Passaic

6 University of Hartford Gym, Hartford

7 Ocean State Theatre, Providence

8, 9 Emerald City, Cherry Hill, NJ

11 Warner Theatre, Washington

12 Palace Theatre, Albany

14, 15 Orpheum Theatre, Boston

17, 18 Agora Ballroom, Atlanta

20 Agora Ballroom, Dallas

21 Armadillo World Headquarters, Austin

22 Agora Ballroom, Houston

1981

January

14 Ulster Hall, Belfast (benefit for Carri Melo)

15, Stardust Ballroom, Dublin

16 Leisureland, Galway

17 UCC Downtown Kampus, Cork

All dates with The Specials

February

5, 12, 19 Ritz, New York

April

21 Rugby, CND Rally

May

2 Sophia Gardens, Cardiff

3 Top Rank, Bristol

4 Rotters, Nottingham

7 De Montfort Hall, Leicester

9 Friars, Aylesbury

11 Victoria Hall, Hanley (cancelled)

12, 13 Locarno, Birmingham

15 University, Lancaster

16 University, Leeds

17 Tiffany's, Glasgow

18 Tiffany's, Edinburgh

21 Apollo, Manchester

22 Royal Court, Liverpool

24 Civic Hall, Wolverhampton

25 Leisure Centre, Gloucester

26 Guildhall, Portsmouth

27 Colosseum, St Austell

31 Rainbow, London

June

1 Hammersmith Palais, London

9 Berlin

Heidelberg cancelled

Nuremburg

Marseille

Lyon (open air)

Amsterdam

July

11 Record *Get Set for Summer*

12 Lisdoonvarna (near Shannon) festival

Cornwall
Bilbao Festival
Imperial Cinema, Birmingham

September
23–30 Théâtre Mogador, Paris (supporting The Clash)

October
16, 17 Masonic Temple, Toronto
19 Vermont
20 The Channel, Boston
21 Browns University, Providence, Rhode Island
23 Ontario Theatre, Washington
24 Ripley's Music Hall, Philadelphia (possibly Emerald City)
26, 27 Ritz, New York
30, 31 Perkins Palace, Los Angeles

November
3, 4 Market St Cinema, San Francisco
25, 26 Bingley Hall, TUC, Rock for Jobs (with UB40)
28 Rainbow, Jobs For Youth campaign

December
11 Victoria Halls, Hanley (rearranged date)
University tour

1982
April
11 Record *Here and Now Special* Roger & Pato

May
Record 'Save It For Later' for *Cheggers Plays Pop*

June
12 Golden Hall, San Diego

13 Mesa Community Center, Phoenix

14–19 Hollywood Palladium, Los Angeles

20 Country Bowl, Santa Barbara

22, 23 Civic Auditorium, San Francisco

All dates with The Clash

July
16–18 Royal Bath and West Showground, WOMAD:

    Friday afternoon outdoor

    Saturday: Showering Pavilion

30 Deeside Leisure Centre, Radio 1 beach party

31 Gateshead International Stadium (supporting The Police, with U2 and Gang Of Four)

August
13 CNE Exhibition Stadium, Toronto, Police Picnic

15 Castle Farms Music Centre, Charlevoix

17 Municipal Auditorium, Nashville

18 Civic Center, Peoria
20 Wisconsin
21 Five Seasons Center, Cedar Rapids
23 Red Rocks Amphitheatre, Morrison
24 Rosenblatt Stadium, Omaha
26 Salt Palace, Salt Lake City
28 Cal Expo Amphitheatre, Sacramento
29 Memorial Coliseum, Portland
31 Pacific Coliseum, Vancouver
All dates with The Police

September
1 Center Coliseum, Seattle
3 Glen Helen Regional Park, San Bernardino
4 Rissmillers, Reseda, CA
5 TCC Arena, Tuscon
6 Pan American Center, Las Cruces
All dates with The Police
7, 8 Orpheum Theatre, Boston (supporting The Clash)
22 Center Arena, Seattle (supporting The Clash)

October
Ulster Hall, Belfast
Tower Ballroom, Birmingham
Hammersmith Palais, London (support from U2)

November
19 Opera House, Boston

20 Ritchie Coliseum, University of Maryland
   (support from The Bangles)
21 Halloran Plaza Ballroom, Philadelphia
24 Nassau Veterans Memorial Coliseum, Uniondale, NY
   (support from REM and Squeeze)
26 Jamaica World Music Festival, Montego Bay, Jamaica
Atlanta, Georgia
29 University of Alabama 'English Beat in Birmingham
   Day', Birmingham
Mississippi riverboat

1983
March
10, 11, 12 Rainbow Music Hall, Denver
26 Page Auditorium, Durham
27 Memorial Hall, Chapel Hill
30 Plaza Hotel, Daytona Beach
31 University of Miami, Coral Gables
All dates with support from REM

April
2 University of the South, Sewanee
5 Vanderbilt Memorial Gym, Nashville
7 Bogart's, Cincinnati
8 University of Kentucky, Lexington
9 Oberlin College, Oberlin
10 Grand Circus Theater, Detroit

12 Alumni Hall, University of Western Ontario

13 University of Rochester, Rochester

14 Buffalo State University, Buffalo

16 Kenyon Hall, Poughkeepsie

17 Le Spectrum de Montréal, Montreal

19 Hamilton College, Clinton

20 Woolsey Hall, New Haven

22 Walter Brown Arena, Boston

23 Agora Ballroom, Hartford

24 Fountain Casino, Aberdeen

26 Spize, Farmingdale

All dates with support from REM

May

North America tour (with support from REM)

28 Glen Helen Regional Park, San Bernardino

June

1 Red Rocks Amphitheatre, Red Rocks Park, Morrison

July

1–3 Milton Keynes Bowl (supporting David Bowie)

ACKNOWLEDGEMENTS

From the outset, Tarquin Gotch had the vision and will to make this book a reality. He has overseen the whole process with grace, generosity and humour. Tarquin's involvement comes with the great support of Holly Topps.

Pauline has been a diamond.

Thanks to Hunt Emerson for the loan of his Beat fanzine collection and always, his great art. And also Terry Stewart.

In the publishing world I am grateful for the backing of David Barraclough, Imogen Gordon Clark, David Stock, Carrie Kania, and the rest of the Omnibus team.

Many thanks to Equilar for reading the first draft and making many necessary corrections. To Susie McDonald for her input on a later draft. And to Nick Jones for overseeing the copy edit.

This book only exists because of the music of The Beat: a huge debt of honour to Dave Wakeling, Andy Cox, David Steele, Everett Morton, Saxa, and Dave Wright.

Finally, a massive thanks to Daniel Rachel without whom I could not have written this book – thanks for his kindness, patience and good humour throughout – I am so proud to share a writing credit with him.

Peace, love and unity – Ranking Roger.